P9-CMY-857

QA
.C66
G3713
1987

	DATE DUE	
MAR 07 1994 S		
OCT 31 1998 S		
DEC 18 1998 S		

The
Third
Apple

The Third Apple

Personal Computers
& the Cultural Revolution

Jean-Louis Gassée

TRANSLATED FROM THE FRENCH BY ISABEL A. LEONARD

HARCOURT BRACE JOVANOVICH, PUBLISHERS

SAN DIEGO   NEW YORK   LONDON

Library of Congress Cataloging-in-Publication Data
Gassée, Jean-Louis.
   The third apple.
   Translation of: La troisième pomme.
   1. Computers and civilization.   I. Title.
QA76.9.C66G3713   1987   303.4'834   86-19557
ISBN 0-15-189850-2

Designed by G.B.D. Smith
Printed in the United States of America
First edition
A B C D E

To Paul, Sophie,
To Brigitte, who made them so beautiful,
And to Seigneur Themouraz,
                              in the shadow

The writer of this poem
Is as dreamy as eternity
As patchy as a quilt
As forgetful as nightmares
As wild as can be.

MAX LAING
July 1984

Contents

CONTENTS

The
Third
Apple

1

A Sonnet in
a Circuit

"NO, I PROMISE, it doesn't bite, it's not expensive, it won't break up your marriage!" I might as well save my breath. They stare at me disbelievingly, thinking I'm something of a charming madman with a strange machine. And, confidentially, they're not altogether wrong. Sometimes I run into them at dinner parties. (It must be said here that though I'm a bit of a stay-at-home, I do yield to mild convivial attractions every now and then.) No sooner do I arrive at one of these parties than I'm hit with a barrage of questions that usually contain some barely veiled reproaches: What are computers good for, anyway? Mankind has gotten along just fine without them for thousands of years, but now they're a must: you've got to learn to use a computer if you want to get ahead, if you don't want to be left behind by history. We poor slobs, despite all our good intentions, are being doomed to suffer the pangs of PC envy. Sure, we want to keep up with the times; but first of all tell us what the damned things are good for! Telephones, okay, we understand them; airplanes and refrigerators too. We can even accept VCRs and compact-disk players. And we're quite willing to admit that *big* computers are essential, if only to send us our bank statements on time. But personal computers for home use—micro-computers—well, we just don't get it.

The first response that comes to my mind in such cases, if these troubled spirits will forgive me, is to speak of the pleasure, even the ecstasy, I experience when I use these modern household gods. The pleasure is ambiguous, I'll readily admit, but is any pleasure ever innocent? We'll leave it to the philosophers to argue over this weighty question and busy ourselves instead with trying to see what the particular pleasure in personal computers is really all about.

Anyone who fearlessly sets himself with an open mind in front of a personal computer will (trust me) sooner or later experience the sense of being on top of the world. He'll be suffused with an extraordinary, euphoric feeling of power. Note that I say *power*, not *authority*. *Power* indicates what I am able to do for myself; *authority* is what I exercise over others. In computer circles, these concepts are at war with each other. On the side of authority are the big main-

4

frames, tended by high priests who possess the essential knowledge and thus a large share of control within the company that employs them. Those who need what the mainframes provide must bow down to these electronic druids who hand down the word of the electronic god. Knowledge, control, authority. . . . On the other side, the side of power, are the personal computers—they hold all the winning cards. When you use a personal computer you enjoy direct access to a machine of power that allows you to play while working, play while learning. In my opinion, by the way, there is nothing more serious than playing. I have a lot of trouble understanding the labored distinction that has been made between work and play. I solemnly swear, with my hand on my heart and my eyes on the gray rectangle of my Apple screen, that this distinction vanished from my life a few years ago. And I'm getting along very nicely without it.

How was this miracle accomplished? You must understand that, like a human being, this inert object covered with plastic, sitting on the table, is not a constant: it takes many forms, it changes, it varies. This multiplicity and flexibility are what make it so seductive. All you have to do is feed it another disk and its personality changes. It's not the same, but it's not really different either. It doesn't look as if it has changed. The plastic-covered object is still there before your eyes, but now that it has a new personality, the things you can do with it are radically different: juggling tables of numbers to work out a budget, or learning to play chess, or programming, composing music, writing a book, trying various combinations of ideas, reading the *Wall Street Journal*, constructing a puzzle, designing a model airplane. To travel from one universe to another, all you have to do is *insert a new disk.*

At these dinner parties, they tell me it's a fad, a temporary fascination with a new type of gadget. Maybe. But some fads last. The pioneers of aviation heard plenty of this kind of talk too, but they started a "fashion" that isn't over yet. With computers, it is thought that takes wing. True, computer illiterates feel that a sort of vast blue sky above separates them from computer literates. There are the computer people and the ignorant laymen, just as there are people who buy their clothes at Yves St. Laurent and the rest of us. The excluded, the laymen, feel left behind, on the ground, frustrated, missing the action going on above them. Moreover, they have a sneaking suspicion that these half-magic, half-devilish machines are much more than a mere fad, that they are indeed a form of power. Their frustration comes from feeling deprived of this singular power, which fascinates and frightens at the same time. Computer science is like electricity—it's both marvelous and dangerous. This new form of energy can shed light and enlighten. But will it also electrocute me? Will it serve me or destroy me? Help me or dominate me? Who will come out on top, the machine or I? This sort of uncertainty has always accompanied scientific progress. People have always been skeptical of inventions that have changed their lives. But the computer makes this anxiety even more acute and disturbing because it does not stop at manipulating electrons or waves: it manipulates thought, transmits it, prolongs it, speeds it up. The big question behind all the others is, Does *it* think? And so, Will *it* take my place? There is no privilege more jealously guarded by men than this astounding faculty of thinking; we fear nothing more than having to share it with other beings. At the same time—read in any number of science-fiction novels—we never cease to imagine robots that think or genius-level extraterrestrials.

This mixture of fascination with and resistance to computers is rather comforting. Each time I'm confronted with it, I tell myself that these passionate reactions prove at least one thing: that I am, as they say, onto a good thing, riding the crest of a ninth wave. Computers—especially microcomputers—leave no one indifferent. They are worshiped or hated, adored or disparaged—with equal vigor. They play a leading role, both symbolic and real, in our universe; and even those who prefer to bury their heads in the sand feel worried, attacked, disconcerted, questioned. Because I have chosen, happily and de-

THE THIRD APPLE

liberately, to link my destiny to that of information science, I am assailed by critics, challenged by the fearful. At dinners where I'm buttonholed by people filled with anguish and painful curiosity, I am no longer simply Jean-Louis Gassée, forty-three years old, vaccinated, married, father of three children, lover of puns, music, and California, curious about rhetoric and psychoanalysis, a voracious magazine reader, a math freak who wandered into the business world. I am, rather, an emanation of Apple; I represent a function, a culture, a technology. I have a little trouble getting used to it. We always prefer to be liked or disliked for ourselves, for the color of our eyes or shoes, for the liveliness of our minds, for the quality of our souls, for the number of our vices. But finally I got used to this strange feeling. No doubt I have not yet entirely succeeded in formulating the convictions that inhabit my days and stand behind all my actions. I hope that writing this book will help me to clarify some things at last, if only for myself. I want this book to be an invitation to voyage into a region of the mind where technology and poetry exist side by side, feeding each other.

So, once more, I'm talking with two voices that are really one: Apple's and my own. I am so closely identified with this company, which is like no other, that I feel I'm speaking for myself when I speak for Apple. I have always worked with computers. I began "for real" at age twenty-four, but in my mind and desires I was at it long before. I always knew I would have a job something like the one I have now. It was quite obvious: I wanted to spend my life in the world of my childhood electric trains. So when I joined Apple six years ago I felt, *This is it, I have arrived.* I was home.

We have two tasks here on earth: to structure our time and to make sense of things. When I joined Apple I immediately felt I was going to participate in an adventure that made more and better sense than any other. Why? First of all, there is the symbol, of course. Our name says it all: the apple, an apple with all the colors of the rainbow. (It was Steve Jobs who threw out the Apple name, just like a child blowing a soap bubble to look at the pretty colors. One day in 1976, when everyone was scratching his head to come up with a name for the new company, he said, "If we haven't got anything by five this afternoon, it'll be Apple Computers." That was one of those lightning intuitions that change many people's destinies. If the company had called itself MBI Computers, it certainly would not have gone through the adventures it has.) In the Old Testament there was the *first apple*, the forbidden fruit of the Tree of Knowledge, which with one taste sent Adam, Eve, and all mankind into the great current of History. The *second apple* was Isaac Newton's, the symbol of our entry into the age of modern science. The Apple Computers symbol was not chosen purely at random:

it represents the *third apple*, the one that widens the paths of knowledge leading toward the future. A symbol is like a pebble you throw in the water: waves form and grow wider as they move away from the center. What is forming and growing around the symbolic apple is desire (perhaps even lust)—but also knowing, understanding, and the sense of drama. The third apple, ours, is a bit tart; it has a special, inimitable flavor. In the industrial adventure of our time, I can hardly think of a single company with a comparable taste. (Of course, this all had to do with the personalities of Apple's two founders: Steve Jobs, that obsessed and charismatic visionary who would have sold his soul to make good products, a fanatic with an impossible disposition; and Steve Wozniak, who represented the gentle side of things, an easygoing, reflective man, the incarnation of simplicity. Fire and water.)

By now you might have guessed that the domain of the computer, for me, is the domain of poetry, the rather special poetry of those who can see a sonnet in a circuit. This sort of poetry eventually emerges through the machine's plastic body. When I got to Apple, I opened an Apple II and saw its disk controller—the internal circuit that connects the computer to the memory stored on an external floppy disk. I was amazed: the computers I knew had floppy-disk controllers about a hundred inches square. But this circuit was minute, only eight to nine inches. I learned later that it was famous in computer circles for the way Wozniak had simplified it and for the new possibilities it offered program users—despite, or because of, this simplicity. Today a Macintosh integrated circuit uses the same ideas. In homage to Wozniak, it is called IWM, Integrated Woz Machine.

I confess that in high school I found and was attracted to the poetry in mathematics, but all the while perversely insisted to my math teacher that I was moved only by the poetry in literature and greatly preferred its richness to the "sterility" of mere numbers. Now I no longer have to express a preference for one or the other, for numbers or art. I choose to have my cake and eat it too. And I am determined that my son also not feel any pressure to choose one over the other. He has had a Macintosh since he was three. When he plays with it, he says, "I'm working."

And when he paints with it, he says, "I see Mac Paint" and busily proceeds to express himself on the screen, though he hasn't yet done the work of learning to read and write. But the point is, you don't have to learn to read and write before you can express yourself with this computer. You can, if you like, read the names of programs, but you can also identify them just as easily by their graphic symbols. With the little instrument we call the mouse, hand-and-eye coordination is literally child's play. My son paints: he chooses the symbol for the paint can, or the broad brush, or the pencil—and then he does what he wants. He manipulates metaphors, and that allows him to create. He has taught me a lot about the way adults relate to the computer. Adults tend to repress their pleasure. Sad to say, I think we become adults only through disappointment, grief, and lies. So of course gradually we become tough, less sensitive. But behind the protective facade is a child. When my son presses the *A* on the keyboard and sees an enormous *A* appear on the screen, he exults and says, "I'm making *A*!" Adults feel the same thing without always showing it, without daring to express their joy. When I let my joy burst forth, people look at me askance. It's not proper.

2

Drinking a Glass

THOSE WHO NAÏVELY IMAGINE that a car is nothing more than a way to get around are deluding themselves. A car, like a computer, is an instrument of liberation. It lets you go where you want without being answerable to anyone and without always having to take the same route. It is a power mediator. I drive to Doue-la-Fontaine the way I want when I want. As I drive, I daydream. I can stop en route if I feel like it and stretch out on the grass. In a similar fashion, my computer lets my mind roam to the ends of the earth. I choose my itinerary, my schedule, my rhythm. I take shortcuts, I go backward, I rush forward. Freedom.

Of course, the analogy does have its limits, which I'll try to explain. I confess to a predilection for fine cars. I admire their comfort, their efficiency, their sleek or majestic lines. But (and here's where the analogy breaks down) I never forget that a car is an object. My relationship with the computer, however, is far more complex. Does it mechanically do what I tell it (him? her?) to do, like an appliance, or does the power it wields change the *quality* of my own thinking?

The fact is that a computer is not just any machine. It may look like a machine, but it belongs to another species altogether. The difference between a computer and an ordinary machine is as vast as the difference that separates invertebrates from primates. The computer is at once a manipulator of symbols and clay for the mind to shape. It extends and enhances the potential of human intelligence.

A good stereo system has more buttons than a Macintosh and looks more sophisticated. But it is used for only one thing—listening. Its function is limited. The computer, though, possesses an aura of openness, of boundless spaces. Why? The software. In an ordinary machine, the software is a given, unalterable, beyond your control. When you choose a stereo, you don't worry about the software—you know that any record will play on it. The same is true of a sewing machine—it can sew any fabric, period. But with a computer the software is much more important: it is both the fuel that drives the machine and the pattern that gives it its character.

A diskette is flat and square and not very impressive, but when it goes to work for you, you get right to the heart of the matter—running the program. We say "running" a program because it runs for a certain time at a certain rhythm, just like a musical score. You can play just one movement if you like, back up, figure something out, reread, and little by little discover subtleties that were imperceptible in the beginning. No wonder many software writers are also musicians.

Poetry and music—these words take us a long way from the distressing image often evoked by the term *computer,* an image left over from the days computers were perceived as mighty demons lurking in the depths of banks and insurance companies. It is an infernal, Plutonian image—one that creates a feeling of heaviness, incomprehensibility, blind financial power struggles. But actually these monsters are quite docile—indeed, they are vegetarians that feed only on paper. We have some at Apple, and they are extremely useful. We would find it hard to do without them; so would a lot of other people. But microcomputers, despite their name, belong to another family. They are lightweight, cheerful, and friendly. If mainframes are associated with Pluto and the Underworld (inevitably implying the death-dealing power of institutional wealth), microcomputers evoke the world of Apollo, of light and lightness, of buoyant individuality. It's the difference between an object that anyone can save up to buy and something that only an institution can afford.

The confusion arises because both machines have the same name: *ordinateur* in French, *computer* (meaning "calculator") in English. The French term is closer to the mark, though, because it emphasizes the idea of creating order. Human intelligence is elastic: it can handle the intuitive and the approximate. If you say to a computer, "I am going to drink a glass," it won't understand you. By computer logic, you don't ever drink a glass, you drink the liquid inside it. If you tell it, "I bought a mink," it'll ask you, "Where's its cage?" This raises the whole problem of artificial intelligence: How do you convert the elastic distortions imposed by language into the binary system used by computers? How do you teach a machine to proceed by approximations?

Because they impose a certain rigid order, computers can help us to understand how we think. What is a concept? It is a path between two other concepts. A new idea is an idea that links two others. But this new path is itself a concept, an idea, a place. How can a path and a place be the same thing? When I ask a colleague to come and drink a glass (of wine, let's say) with me, I am effecting a double transformation: I am transforming the idea of glass—the material—to designate the drinking vessel made of glass, and I am transforming it a second time to designate the contents of the glass. There is nothing easier than tripping up a computer—all you have to do is feed it a list of idioms or read it a poem. It will be able to check that a line of verse has ten syllables; it could even check the rhymes. But if you ask, "Is this good poetry? Does it mean anything? Is it beautiful?" it will be quite incapable of giving you the right answers. A computer is totally disarmed by a riddle or crossword-puzzle definition. How could it understand that "Man" is the answer to "What goes on four feet, on two feet, and three / But the more feet it goes on the weaker it be"? How could it comprehend that the nineteenth hole is really the bar of the country club? This limitation of computers pinpoints something about the specific nature of human intelligence. Computers fascinate me because they teach me who I am.

3

In the Bridal Suite
at the Hilton

FOR ME, A TRIP TO CALIFORNIA always meant a return to the source of the legend. After a while I would get nostalgic and sense the need to immerse myself in the myth again. In February 1981 I felt this need. In those days I was working for the East Coast companies, and my last pilgrimage to Silicon Valley had been as far back as 1973 when I was at Hewlett-Packard, a company founded by another pair of inventors who, like Jobs and Wozniak, began in a garage. So I was happy to be back in the Hilton, on the famous Route 101 that links San Francisco with Los Angeles. I don't know why, but I was assigned the bridal suite. When I opened the door I found out just how bad American kitsch could be: chiné cretonne with long acrylic fibers, electric colors, and

23

worst of all a huge four-poster bed. I had just escaped from Sheraton's "ancient castle" (built all the way back in 1965!), which lords it over the Massachusetts Turnpike. I was overwhelmed. I had the privilege of playing quietly in the ugliest luxury in the world. But it was not until I sat on the bed and looked up that I really knew how lucky I was: the canopy was faced with a Mylar mirror, that flexible metallized plastic which deforms what it reflects.

It was in this inimitable decor that I married Visicalc. I had managed to kidnap an Apple II to install in the room. After plugging it in, I duly *booted*—a sacred term in our jargon that comes from "bootstrap." It is a metaphor which simply means that to run the machine's big program you have to wake it up with a smaller program—a sort of loader—written on a diskette. In practice, this means that you insert a diskette into the drive, just as you insert a cassette into a tape recorder. After a few fruitless attempts, caused by compatibility problems that I'll come back to later, I succeeded for the first time in getting Visicalc up and running. I must confess, by the way, that the nuptial decor in which this event took place gave it additional meaning: people who live in intimate contact with these funny machines have the strange habit of talking about them in sexual metaphors. There is a tradition among system programmers, the pros among pros, that involves revealing their sense of humor in the comments they write in the margins of printouts. These are documents that remain private, giving them a rather astonishing freedom of tone and vocabulary. But freedom is not always synonymous with variety, and they are often confined to science fiction and the salacious. No Elizabethan poetry. . . . And the programmers, even when they are women, don't surprise anyone when they call their machines "bitches."

So Visicalc offered itself to me on the screen: a sheet of ruled paper with rows and columns. Little by little I noticed that this program, which looked like nothing in particular, allowed three budget simulations (something every company head needs but never has the time or courage to do) to be executed in two steps. With a family budget, for example, you might ask what would be the overall effect of an unexpected expense in February: you add 8 percent to the appropriate column and the calculations for the entire year are changed in an instant. A single item changes and everything is recalculated. A pebble is thrown into a pond, and all the shock waves appear on the screen.

I couldn't believe my eyes. I was all the more astounded because it was exactly what I had tried to do ten years earlier, when I was sales manager at Hewlett-Packard France. At the time, I sweated blood over big green sheets with twelve columns, plus one at the left for the items and one on the right for the totals. I should have felt honored at having to do this piece of work: preparing a budget is a status symbol. But it would never come out right; the totals wouldn't match. And then, if I felt like changing one assumption, I had to start again from the top. I had machines, of course, but they worked only one row at a time. To escape this slave labor, I toyed with the idea of programming a simulation array to integrate rows and columns. But I had to admit that my budget-programming career would soon come to a halt. It was a Chinese puzzle; and at the time we didn't have the tools necessary to invent Visicalc. I gave up and found other jobs where there would be someone to do the calculating drudgery for me.

So Visicalc was the thing I had dreamed of making ten years earlier. I had dreamed it, imagined it, and there it was in my room. This happens all the time in our business: dreams become realities and new thoughts follow on their heels. Sometimes you even find yourself with an invention you weren't aware you'd dreamed of, but you *recognize* it. It is through revelations like that one that the market develops.

Visicalc is a network, a three-dimensional calculator: rows, columns, and lurking at every intersection between row and column, behind each "cell," a formula that weaves the links between the formulas. This is the structure of the model that Visicalc recalculates every time a change is introduced, every time a pebble is thrown into the pond. At home, Visicalc can be used to work out the budget; it can help a financial manager prepare his operating account, a publisher prepare the launching of his list, a treasurer try cash-flow assumptions—it is a three-dimensional calculator. Most important of all, it adds an essential dimension: simulation. In fact, the creators of Visicalc, two young men from the East Coast, Dan Bricklin and Bob Frankston, had invented it for the same reasons that led me to imagine it: they had had enough of redoing calculations fifty times that a machine should have done so much better, but couldn't.

That was the day I realized that you didn't have to be a programmer any more to use a computer. Visicalc was a phenomenal revolution. Until it appeared you had to learn a language—Basic, Pascal, Fortran, Cobol, or Lisp. You had to pass through a whole series of chambers before entering the majestic room where the computer was enthroned. The Moloch was surrounded by high priests in white jackets, the only ones who understood the text of the incantations addressed to the machine god whose bowels contained the programs. It was fed with punched cards and excreted the results in the form of printouts. There were three distinct stages: input, processing, output.

But with Visicalc this hierarchy disappeared. Exchange, dialogue, and interaction are continuous. Not only is the instrument available at any moment in anyone's office; not only does it use simple metaphors—a sheet with rows and columns—and proceed by known elementary operations—subtraction, multiplication, etc.—but it gives results instantaneously and can modify them over and over again. Instead of compelling the user to adapt to the machine and talk its language, the machine bends to his needs—his desires!—and speaks his language. Visicalc displays the data and the results at the same time; it abolishes the unnatural act of hierarchic thinking that distinguishes between the data and the structure of the model. It makes them both equally accessible to handling by the user. Thus we escape the digestive metaphor of Moloch. No longer do we have to learn a new language; we don't even have to figure out in advance what we're going to do.

Visicalc confirms what artificial-intelligence specialists discovered by complicated reasoning: human intelligence functions in a muddled sort of way, by approximation and by constructing tangled hierarchies. When you think, you don't know what you're doing, you don't know where you're going; you have to be free to be wrong, to play with numbers and formulas, to stroll from one end of a path of reasoning to another. Visicalc respects this need, and this is its heuristic genius (heuristics: the art of good discovery): I can get where I want to go even if I didn't know where I was going when I started. So it's a tool that allows you, in an area reputed to be dull, to maintain the natural sequence of thinking ("I think that's how it is; let's check. My data are wrong? No problem, I'll start over. And over. And over . . ."). Approximations, trial and error, simulations—Visicalc is an intellectual modeling clay. It lets you program without knowing it. Whether you think so or not, programming is an essential life-skill: cooking, writing dates in a diary, that's programming. The question is not whether you're going to program with a computer, but what method and what intellectual objects, endowed with what power, you're going to use to program.

It's also a communication tool. When a financial manager has finished his budgetary ruminations, he doesn't stop there: he must convince his boss, his colleagues, and his clients. Of course he could just print out his finished table on a transparency and project it on a screen. But in a company meeting, comments on a table of figures are likely to bore everyone to tears. In particular, you are likely to miss seeing the forest for the trees in a bunch of figures, overlooking what really counts: trends, relationships between phenomena, *shapes*. What counts is not a series of percentages but the general upward or downward pattern.

A more-or-less ordinary human brain has trouble converting liters per hundred kilometers into miles per gallon: there is a change in equations and a change in units at the same time. A computer does this calculation easily. By contrast, the human brain sees shapes very well. Visicalc was quickly supple-

mented with another program called Visiplot. And
now we have Multiplan and Chart and integrated
programs such as Excel and Jazz. Their original fea-
ture was to translate arrays of numbers into graphs
and pictures with reliefs, colors, and perspectives.
These pictures create meaning, they tell a story, they
have a power of expression infinitely superior to any
table of figures. The image goes straight to the point;
it transmits an instantaneous message. It is also possible, when you want to perk up a text, to illustrate
it with drawings, as copyist monks in the pre-Guten-
berg days so felicitously did with their illuminations.
Their talent atrophied when the invention of printing, which mechanized work, reduced the number of
characters available to typographers. But today things
are turning around: mechanization has become sophisticated enough, flexible enough, for it to be possible to bring back the abandoned signs. And they
can be manipulated by the most skeptical adult. To
add pictures to a computer printout you don't have
to have taken twenty years of calligraphy with a Zen
master.

Of course, the computer can also be used to lie.
There are four canonical forms of the lie: commis-
sion, omission, statistics, graphs. And now there is
also Visicalc. We tend to take everything that comes
out of the computer as gospel truth. They used to
say, "I read it in the paper" or "I heard it on TV."
Today we place our confidence in the computer. This

confidence may be a little excessive. The computer is only a tool, a mediator: if the data it has been given are wrong, the output will be meaningless. As we say in the computer vernacular, GIGO (Garbage In, Garbage Out).

As for graphs, they have a particular propensity to distort reality: using the same figures, you can construct two graphs with contradictory meanings. According to the first, everything is fine. According to the second, the company is courting disaster. By playing with scales or methods of extrapolation, you can swallow up whole investment budgets or show that segments of the market are about to explode. Nothing is easier than to distort the message transmitted by a computer. Let me stress this point: discernment remains an essential virtue that no tool, not even Visicalc, can replace.

When I was young, I was an avid reader of A. E. Van Vogt—and thus of the theories of Korzybski, the basis of which is the following: the map is not the land itself. Every time you take a step forward, you walk on this idea—it's almost terrifying, because it sets the limits of representing reality. Democracies know this: there is no representation without a lie. We are condemned to live in this existential lie. We can't check our own names every five minutes. The danger of graphic representation and the distortions it brings about is a particular case of this contradiction between the picture and the actual object.

But let's get back to the discussion of the company. The financial manager is proposing a budget with 6 percent earmarked for public relations. They're going through a tough patch, however, and his boss thinks that 4.5 percent would be more reasonable. No problem: during the coffee break he goes back to his office, changes the assumption, and voilà! the whole table is changed.

Life is not made up of sudden, cathartic decisions. You make tiny decisions every instant, throughout the thinking process. Personal computers cannot be used to make decisions: they assist in thinking; they save time and free the mind by making several complicated calculations at once; they supply the data that allow you to proceed by trial and error before deciding. By taking on the most cumbersome tasks, they extend the possibilities of human thought and usher in a new form of division of labor.

With computers, you can engage in five kinds of normal activities: thinking, organizing, communicating, learning, and playing. But it's different: these activities are made easier and more fun. They allow us to do the things we did before more often and better. The things we can't do for lack of time or knowledge, out of intellectual inhibition or fear, they allow us to taste, thereby giving us a powerful motivation to dare to accomplish them. As for the things we don't know how to do, they show us we *can* do them. Like the Baron of Serendipe in a Voltaire story, we make "happy and unexpected discoveries." *Serendipity.* I know of no better word to suggest the joys of working with a personal computer.

You'll see the old association between work and unhappiness fade away—mark my words.

4

The Risk of the Winds

WHAT IS AN ENTREPRENEUR? Someone who wants to live on through his work, who is prepared to generate a new being, to take risks. For an entrepreneur to do what he does, unless he has a personal fortune, he needs someone to support him, to take risks with him, to taste the adventure. That is the role of the venture capitalist.

I have had the good fortune to know two civilizations, that of France and that of California. One cannot compare old Europe, with its discreet charms and measured joys, to the West Coast, with its futuristic attractions and brassy hedonism. But for desire, adventure, enterprise in the fullest sense of the word, there is nothing like the pioneering spirit.

Is it reasonable to believe that desire can be created by decree? In France they keep telling us in every tone of voice: we have to create our own Silicon Valley; we need entrepreneurs. Nothing easier, says the government, you just have to have the will. We have plenty of enlightened financiers who will fuel the enterprise for you; just go and see them, propose a project; you'll see, they're waiting for you. Our banks contain sleeping venture capital just waiting for someone to wake it up. Gentlemen, entrepreneurs: on your marks, get set, go with your ideas.

Okay. Let's play along and see what happens. Sincerely, naïvely. Suppose I want to set up a software publishing company. The market exists, the writers are raring to go, the idea is a good one, the business plan is written. A solid project, ready to launch.

With my business plan in my briefcase, I go to the Paribas Bank (one of the largest banks in France), where my sage advisers have told me there is venture capital for sale. I am received with every courtesy; I talk about my idea, the stages of the project, the market situation. And I point out that I need twelve million francs to get started.

Before continuing this story, let's digress for a moment. Under the same circumstances, with the same project, what would happen in California? I would go to see one of the numerous venture capital firms or one of the independent financiers who ply this trade as solitary navigators. They would reply:

"One million eight hundred thousand dollars? That's all? Are you sure your estimates aren't a bit tight?" And my venture capitalist would explain with a broad smile that the primary cause of death of new businesses, especially in infancy, is lack of capital. You have to think big; nothing is more dangerous than underestimating your needs. "Your idea is a good one, you have experience, I can deal with you. But why don't you take $2 million. . . . And now let's talk about the second round of financing you'll need, especially when you're in a growth phase. A business that succeeds will eat up a lot of money before it brings any in. . . ." This is the story venture capitalists tell entrepreneurs in the Valley. Under what conditions will the business be set up? They are very simple: the capitalist supplies 100 percent of the capital but contents himself with 60 percent or so control of the business and allows the entrepreneurs 40 percent. "So, if it takes off, you will participate in the success of the business by owning something that'll become more and more valuable." It sounds like a dream.

Let's come back to earth, i.e., at Paribas. What do the enlightened financiers of this great bank tell me? "Your idea's great, we'd give a lot to see experienced entrepreneurs like you more often, your business plan is excellent, you know the market. Well done!" But they will ask to look over a few details. Nobody's perfect. . . . French banks are peopled with graduates of technical institutes who come by way of the National Fuel Directorate and who, although they have only the vaguest notions about the microcomputer market, pride themselves on being familiar with every facet of the economy.

These reasonable people would not have taken the exorbitant risk of giving money to an inexperienced nineteen-year-old like Steve Jobs to help him start a company called Apple. There are dozens of young people like Jobs in Paris today. Where can they go? Why does it have to be us, Apple, who help a twenty-three-year-old man, Luc Barthelet, to make a fortune by selling fifteen thousand copies of the program he invented for spreadsheets all by himself, in his little corner, the best now on the market, now sold worldwide for the Apple II? But to continue . . .

Then those same bankers will ask me another professorial question: "Are you sure that in five years the market will develop in this direction?" Of course I'm not sure; I can't read the stars. If you think about it, how could a venture capitalist ask such a question? How can he demand that risk be eliminated when his job consists precisely of taking risks? The only question should be "Is it a good risk?" Beginning with this type of question, you can talk seriously, weigh the pros and cons, and examine the various possible market patterns by taking the unpredictable into account. Once the preliminaries are over, they tell me:

"Okay, you'll have your twelve million francs to get started." I am very happy, but I ask how the shares will be distributed. "What distribution? You're not contributing any money, so you have no capital. You'll have zero percent of the capital. Very simple. If you insist, we'll give you a seat on the board of directors." In other words, my desire, my idea, my experience, my knowledge of the market—all of this together— has no market value because it isn't *capital*.

In France we have difficulty rewarding contributions made by penniless entrepreneurs. It's not part of our culture. To make money you have to have money. But if French bankers play venture capitalist without the entrepreneurs participating in the fruits of their enterprise, they're giving them a raw deal. For entrepreneurs, sharing goes without saying, or it should. But why not do the same with employees? Why not make the offer to newly hired workers that over four or five years they can acquire growing portions of a block of shares in the company, at a price set in advance? In this way, if they participate in the company's growth, they will own shares whose value is greater than the price at which they were purchased. So they know they'll get a good deal if they do their best for the company. Everyone knows that what is called participation as it has been practiced since de Gaulle is more of a farce than an economic stimulus. Unfortunately, this simple idea gets bad press in France, particularly among those whose job it is to care for the well-being of employees. It is one of the great paradoxes of union activity in France: equity and profit sharing organized on a large scale could be both an economic stimulus, creating jobs, and a significant factor in raising the standard of living of workers. But that's where the shoe pinches. The hard-line Left thinks it needs workers to be unhappy to get their votes. It is well known that the Communist Party and the CGT [the French union linked to the Communists] in particular have always been opposed to equity and profit sharing. This refusal cannot be explained by their avowed objectives: improving the standard of living of their members. But the rank-and-file are also voters, and it is traditionally the damned of the earth who vote for these institutions, so damned they must stay. If the damned turned into partners, there would have to be an ideological and electoral revolution. Just the same, I would remind you that the largest stockholders on the New York Stock Exchange are none other than the pension funds of American workers.

Truth in the New World, error in the Old. Some time ago, Paribas was authorized by the French Treasury Department to export $50 million to invest in Silicon Valley. How does Paribas function in California? Exactly like the American venture capitalists: by offering 40 percent or so of the capital to the entrepreneurs. So a nationalized bank has been transformed into a wholly owned venture capitalist that treats American entrepreneurs better than French entrepreneurs. It is true that they could do nothing else; if they didn't play the game, no one in the United States would want their money. I should add, however, that the Paribas money—French taxpayers' money—goes through the hands of a Boston manager as soon as it touches New World soil, and he automatically takes a percentage. So when Paribas starts doing business in the Valley, it has to put up with 50 to 60 percent control of its initial capital instead of the 100 percent it considers its due in Paris.

The first to make use of venture capital were the Lombard bankers of the thirteenth century who financed merchant ships. If the cargo came safely into port, the bankers shared the profits with the captain. If the galleon was shipwrecked, the financiers lost their entire stake. It was an adventure, a risk of the winds, a risk of disaster. They took it with their eyes open.

Unfortunately, in France the words *adventure*—and the word that derives from it, *venture*—and *capital* seem to have incompatible meanings. Furthermore, it is the spirit of enterprise itself that is perceived as an unseemly passion, a little bit like the time when an aristocrat could not get his hands dirty doing business. By definition, an entrepreneur is success-oriented, or failure-oriented, just because he does not sit with his arms folded. And if the French have an exaggerated contempt for those who fail, they do not have an equivalent admiration for those who succeed.

In France, failure is a no-no; if you go bankrupt, it proves you're a deadbeat and no one will trust you. But here is another way to look at things. In Silicon Valley if you fail the first time, they think you've learned something and will be more careful next time around. If you come up with a new project, they'll listen to you attentively. "Nothing ventured, nothing gained," the saying goes, and failure is part of apprenticeship in business life, a normal and even desirable stage in the life of an entrepreneur—not to say in the life of a man. You have to learn how to fall off a horse to become a good rider. Errors and scars are part of this cardinal virtue they call experience. As a result, in Silicon Valley, when three engineers go off for a beer after work, they discuss what kind of deal they can cut to set up a new company. They know they'll probably get the financing, and they know they're allowed to be wrong.

This is not the case in France. Once you've failed, you're dead; no one will lend you a cent. But if you succeed, it's almost worse: you're probably untrustworthy, maybe a crook. It's as if success, instead of being a way to create wealth, were just a clever way to separate other people from their money. Remember the old story of the two ties. A mother offers her son a red tie and a blue tie. The son happily tries on the red one, whereupon the mother dissolves into tears: "I just knew you wouldn't like the blue one!" This is what psychologists call a double bind, something that gets us coming and going in France. It is why, for some obscure reason, money makes us feel uncomfortable.

One current that runs through French thinking is a stubborn prejudice that sees money as an instrument of oppression. Of course it *can* be, under some circumstances, but it is also the fuel of business and the language of success. Money is only a medium. It has no identity per se; it becomes what you decide to do with it. Odd that in France it's considered more respectable to inherit a fortune than to create one. Even if a father builds his fortune on a shady basis, his son will nonetheless be a respected heir. Death seems to have the ambiguous merit of purifying money, giving it illusory virginity. Why is a dead man's money honored more than that of a living man? Perhaps this strange system of prejudices is left over from the old French fascination with the aristocracy. Who is a count, after all? A viscount who took the trouble to get born and whose father died, not a man who worked toward a goal.

The contempt of the French for money is probably the measure of the fears—and hence the desires—that it inspires in them. But if you want to motivate people to take risks, if you want to lead all those executives simmering under the protective lid of nationalized companies out into the big wide world to create new products and high-performance companies, you have to give them models. You have to change the image of the entrepreneur, give him back his titles to fame, his right to make mistakes, and his venturesome spirit. It won't be the few tax incentives, rather paltry ones, we enjoy today that will accomplish the miracle of changing our ways. As long as contributions to industry go unrewarded, as long as a good idea is not nourished with capital, as long as wage earners are sheltered from the ups and downs of the economy, things will not change, all the fine speeches and good intentions notwithstanding.

In the areas of money, success, and fortune, the behavior of our fellow citizens is confined in a corset of traditions and prejudices handed down to us by the ages. When you ask bankers why they decide not to share equity with entrepreneurs, they reply that the laws forbid it. Come on now! Since when have bankers let themselves be ruled by legislation? Laws only follow customs; we have seen this in recent years particularly as regards laws on family and sex. There's nothing *intrinsically* good or bad about money; it's not a devil—it's a tool, an instrument that only has those good and bad qualities we ascribe to it. I'd be the first to agree that it's time for the French to make up their minds to take risks. But before that's going to happen, they're going to have to agree to honor success. And stop being ashamed of wanting it. They will have to change or renegotiate their perverse deal with death and learn to value the fruits of life without waiting for death to sanitize them.

5

A Scent of the Infinite

ONE MONDAY IN DECEMBER 1980, at 1:00 P.M., Tom Lawrence asked me to set up the French subsidiary of Apple. I didn't hesitate for a second, because I knew right away that we'd get along. Tom Lawrence, the man they call "Lawrence of Europe" or "The Great White Father," was formerly Intel's general manager in Europe, a true captain of industry, one in a million. Apple Europe was his "baby": he had created it out of nothing, and now he was offering me the chance to create another baby. There was no doubt in my mind that we could work together. At 7:00 A.M. on Thursday morning we reached an agreement, and by Friday evening, in Geneva, I had signed my contract. I have the happiest memories of this meeting; the important decisions in my life have frequently been made almost automatically, with the same simplicity and clarity.

I had only a vague idea of what I was getting into, and I certainly didn't know how fast I was going to have to shed some old ideas. I had worked in companies like Hewlett-Packard and Data General, and I was at the time managing the Exxon Office Systems subsidiary. From pocket calculators to "megaminis," from scientific to business computers, from OEM (original equipment manufacturers) sales to banking applications, I had seen the computer field from many angles. But I reeked of office automation when I left Paris.

I had to start shifting gears as soon as I reached Cupertino, California, where I was to meet my new bosses—and where, in my room at the Hilton, I was going to marry Visicalc. The first question that came to my mind, of course, was, "Do your machines do word processing too?" Right away my new colleagues, just a little shaken up, proudly presented me with AppleWriter. To my shame, I must confess that this initial contact was a great disappointment.

By comparison with the machines I was used to selling, AppleWriter seemed incredibly primitive. It didn't let you make beautiful displays, and the range of fonts was limited; it let you write but had none of the refinements that turn plain writing into elegant correspondence. A little disdainfully I muttered, "You call that thing a word processor?" But the answer gave me pause: "Yes, sir! We've already sold fifty thousand!" My jaw dropped. The monthly sales rate was far higher than that for all the office-automation workstations at the time.

That was when I became aware of a misunderstanding that, in some companies, has hampered the development of personal computers. I was one of many at the time who did not see that a change was under way. On the one hand, mature companies were selling classical machines, and on the other—people selling gateways to infinity. And even if, in terms of word processing, the performance of the computers could not hold a candle to that of the dedicated word processors, customers preferred them. There were two main reasons for this: first, they were more user-friendly; second and more important, word processing was only one of their functions. The customers wanted this whiff of the infinite that no typewriter, even one with a lot of fancy keys, can give you. Still used to talking in office-automation terms, I had not yet caught on to the radical distinction between a machine and a computer.

AppleWriter became for a time the best-selling software for Apple. There have been many modifications since, but the basic principle remains the same: I turn on the computer, I insert a diskette, I shut the door . . . and there's a sheet of electronic paper. A special kind of paper, on which I can write any way I want, even if I'm not a skilled typist. The screen is like a blank page. After an hour, you completely forget it's a screen. You work away, thinking of nothing else; you can edit, insert, and modify indefinitely—just as you can with the Visicalc spreadsheet.

Rarely is anyone driven by infallible inspiration to write finished copy the first time around. Usually you hesitate, try something, cross it out, go back, fiddle around, and start again. Writing is a trial-and-error business, and word processing allows you to hesitate, rewrite, and edit. Deletions are invisible, paragraphs slide around in space, errors don't matter. Once the document is done, it can be saved on disk, printed, sent by telephone to a correspondent, and so on. If you want to, you can even do programming without knowing computer language. And you can do all that at home just as easily as in your office.

Just as the way switching musical instruments changes the interpretation of a work, writing on a word processor changes the way you write. You can write page after page without worrying about carriage returns and without fear of errors, because errors can be corrected ad infinitum; this gives you an extraordinary sense of freedom. The machine itself ceases to be an obstacle, because you just forget about it. There is nothing more discreet than a good personal computer.

It is essential to understand that word processing on personal computers was invented because the programmers wanted it for themselves. Because they were both programmers *and* users, they created the tools they needed. Wordstar, the ancestor of Apple-Writer and the first in a long line of word-processing software, was originally intended for a population of specialists who had strange tastes for codes. It took dozens of hours to learn to use them. Very soon, though, this instrument with its immense possibilities broke out of the closed circle of techies. AppleWriter and especially MacWrite, the Macintosh word-processing program, represent a decisive step forward because it only takes a few hours to master them; you don't have to learn a new language. Their capabilities are far greater, too. So you can do more while knowing less, which is one definition of pleasure. Beyond these simple applications, AppleWriter also allows you, once you know a few of its secrets, to write a program permitting text-processing pyrotechnics that will satisfy the most demanding user. AppleWriter and Wordstar are, of course, only two examples of a whole category of products from which everyone can choose whatever suits him best.

At the present time, sales of personal computers are far above those of office automation. The office automation company that's doing best, Wang, sells highly elaborate, complex, and efficient systems. But generally it's simplicity that pays off. The spread of computer word processing has resulted in a transformation of the concept of productivity to which office automation is still linked. Of course productivity is a fundamental concept for automobile workers, for example, who are asked to assemble as many cars as possible for the least possible cost, just the way Charlie Chaplin tightened nuts in *Modern Times*. Parenthetically, it is surprising that the Little Tramp, symbolizing the worst aspects of the assembly line, was chosen to advertise a company that is a humanistic one in every other way, I think.

We are still laden with productivity metaphors that correspond to the economic realities of yesterday. For decades, the push was for output: the function of human beings was to produce a certain number of objects in a certain amount of time and for a certain sum of money. But this is no longer the case.

The reason we're so worried about the Japanese challenge is because Japan has shown that the quality of objects counts for just as much as their bottom-line cost. Contrary to popular belief, the average wage in Japan is not significantly less than in Western countries. The Japanese offer products at competitive prices because their manufacturing methods, tools, robots, and employees add up to higher quantity and quality for each unit of wages and capital outlay. It is also because the cost of capital formation is lower. And it is because they offer fewer options. The fact that they produce fewer different model versions of an automobile saves them eight hundred dollars per car.

There are 65,000 different models of the Ford Thunderbird, a fine American car: colors, seats, air conditioners, radios, leather upholstery, dashboards, fenders, wheels, trim—they're all options. This figure, which appears astronomical at first sight, is arrived at very quickly: seven different options for three items adds up to 243 options. With powers of seven you soon reach 100,000. The Japanese limit these choices by trying very intelligently to predict customer preference, thereby lowering their costs. On the other hand, they do not make the mistake of cutting cost by cutting quality; if the customer is dissatisfied, this type of economizing ends up being very expensive. Why do Western consumers buy Japanese VCRs? Because they don't break down. And Japanese cars sell well because they are reliable—and good-looking, too.

In California in 1985, Honda dealers could sell *above list* because their cars were so much in demand. This brings us to another paradox, that of protectionism. Because of the "voluntary" limit on imports, the Japanese can sell at high prices (thanks to quality) in the United States, so they can rake in huge profits, which allow them to invest in factories on American soil and get into the market at the other end. Honda and Nissan are doing it already. Toyota and Mitsubishi are taking another tack: industrial alliances with General Motors and Chrysler. The

Toyota–GM plant in Fremont, California, is next door to the ultramodern plant that assembles the Macintosh. Symbolic?

Productivity, if we take it to mean an obsession with large quantities, is not an operative concept in intellectual professions and in the service and communication sectors. In publishing, productivity does not mean producing the longest possible text in the shortest possible time, but producing something people will want to read. In a manufacturing plant, if you step up productivity you end up in the long run by building robots. In a tertiary company (that is, a company that provides services and distribution), stepping up productivity means the opposite: multiplying human relationships. So we at Apple are not engaged in selling as many machines as possible, but in disseminating high-quality information, allowing our dealers to offer machines that suit the customers who want them.

As you might suspect, word processing is only one way the computer can be used for intellectual work. The next stage is nothing less than processing *ideas*. The programmers who invented ThinkTank are geniuses. I use it every day, whenever I have to present a development program, prepare a speech, or gather my thoughts—which have a natural tendency to scatter; I don't operate like a computer. ThinkTank is a tool for thinking, for constructing plans, synopses, reports. It lets you nest your ideas in each other and keep track of the links between them. With ThinkTank, I imagine I'm playing Tarzan of the Jungle, swinging from idea to idea instead of from tree to tree.

This program respects the complex relationships that lie between thought and writing. As you write, you sense an apparently clear and well-formed thought developing, changing, growing—or maybe being not even worth writing down. New ideas arise in disorderly fashion; you feel the need to jot them down quickly to put them on hold, then shuffle them around. For example, when you're writing a speech, an essay, or the outline of a book, it's useful to have devices that let you manipulate ideas in all directions without their getting entangled, letting them follow their natural course, developing without blocking each other.

ThinkTank lets you save an idea related to Visicalc, for example, in a chapter on spreadsheets, or in a chapter on software writers. You can hesitate, change your mind, or start over as often as you like. Or—somewhat like word processing, which lets you write without worrying about mistakes because you can always correct them later—ThinkTank lets you think in disorderly fashion, by association of ideas. If a paragraph is in the wrong place, I can move it, put it higher or lower in the idea tree. I can also write a paragraph under a chapter heading, hide it, and call it up again when I need it. At the outset, though, I let the ideas flow as they come, in the natural interplay between thinking and writing that lets you invent. ThinkTank respects this movement; you might even say it's *too* flexible because you can keep tinkering with it indefinitely and never be satisfied if you're a perfectionist. This clever invention lets you write a ten-page synopsis in a few hours. You see, personal computers have the two cardinal virtues of tolerance and simplicity.

The role of computer designers is to make innovation an everyday occurrence. I've been using ThinkTank for a long while, and I still marvel each time I use it. I know there'll be other inventions and that once again I'll feel this odd sensation of reliving a forgotten dream. In this field, there's no danger of innovation drying up, if only because the computer is an infinite meta-medium whose possibilities we're just beginning to explore.

In truth, no one really needs a computer until the day he gets one. Then he usually can't do without it. That is what has happened in this century with many inventions. In the industrial society, a new object that invades the market is an object people needed without knowing it. Did nineteenth-century man need antibiotics? I defy anyone to say he didn't. Without knowing it, he needed a drug that didn't exist. Do we need automobiles, telephones, or paperbacks? The ambiguity arises because the problem is wrongly stated—because of the confusion between needing and wanting. A car isn't used just to get around, any more than a library is used merely to store books or a stereo system only to listen to sounds: a car is used to move around *freely*, a library is for *reading*, a stereo is for listening to *music*. Economists should look a little more closely into desire and pleasure, without which there'd be no progress, without which personal computers would never have become these little jewels that have turned work into a game.

It is probable that specialized office-automation machines will continue to develop and become more sophisticated, and that they will end up resembling (to the point of being mistaken for) personal computers. The lesson of this story is that markets arose through companies that listened to their customers. They understood—without always knowing that they had understood, hence their difficulty in making a second product—that it was time to make computers that could serve everyone, not only secretaries but also those who deal in knowledge, i.e., who create, handle, and transmit information.

Secretaries have had their roles broadened and their jobs expanded. Now that they're not the only ones working at a keyboard, they accomplish new tasks, much more interesting ones than dealing with mounds of mail. At Apple there is a computer on every desk: we have forbidden the use of typewriters. The secretaries have different duties, which cover all the jobs that crop up daily in the company. The computers are there to help all of us work the way we want. The job of a secretary is to take over as much of the boss's work as possible. Secretaries get paid less; that's economic efficiency. But the boundary between their work and that of the boss is flexible: their job is interesting, has a future and a chance at a higher salary, and increases the boss's efficiency. The boss in turn can grow on the job and even relax the boundary between himself and *his* boss. I'm willing to bet that no secretary who has been exposed to this work philosophy will want to go back to the old way of doing things.

The computer business, because it is an island of prosperity, serves as a laboratory for innovation in the internal relationships of a company. When I hire people, I explain how we work and then I ask them: "Do you want to hire me as your employer?" It's not a figure of speech. In our business, contracts are by mutual agreement, and power relationships are not unequal; computer people know they can find work elsewhere.

When I made computers mandatory for everyone at AppleFrance, from secretaries to executives, I banned training courses at the same time. No time was to be wasted learning new languages. What happened? Information, instead of staying locked in manuals or remaining the private property of a "knowledge clergy," began to flow in all directions. One of our bearded gurus began to write software explaining how to use the computer. A small culture developed, and everyone started swapping tricks with his neighbor. To think that sociologists have worked out complicated theories to show that the computer contributes to social isolation! How wrong can you be?

6

Is Gossip Dead?

BEFORE THE END OF THIS CENTURY, the computer industry will have become more important than the automobile industry. I really fail to see how this development will keep people apart and condemn them to solitary confinement; quite the contrary. This idea of social atomization as a consequence of the information society may well be widespread, but it's far from the truth.

When personal computers have really become part of everyday life, restaurateurs will spend less time on purchasing and will be more available to look after their customers. Secretaries will stop wearing themselves out on mechanical tasks and will take on new responsibilities in the company. Town clerks will no longer have to search through dusty files and will instead spend their time improving the quality of administrative services. These little changes should come about in every sector of the economy. With little or no flag-waving, almost imperceptibly, they will eventually change the quality of life. I'd really rather not stand in line at the bank to get cash from a grumpy teller when there's a money machine outside the bank. The sweet–sour exchange with employees overtaxed by the unending line of people all asking for the same thing is not a human encounter that interests me. I can do very well without it. But if I want my banker to help me choose the best type of account, I'll gladly make an appointment to see him and discuss it in privacy. Using computers should enable us to shed the routine tasks that obviously fail to stretch our capacities to the full and that generate both bitterness and boredom.

If, however, you listen to some of modern society's experts, you'll hear exactly the opposite. One, for example, says that all sectors of human activity that used to be an occasion for meeting and chatting, for "conviviality," as they say, will tend to be replaced through technical progress by products that sterilize human relationships and that will gradually usher in a civilization of solitude. The classic example is that the supermarket has replaced the butcher, baker, and milkman, so women no longer spend their days exchanging gossip. But then, they don't spend all their time trekking from shop to shop, either. Some people also maintain that computers in schools will spell the end of the educational dialogue between teacher and student. These people don't know that computers are no more capable than books of supplanting this relationship. But they *can* bring about a new form of division of labor between master and machine, with the machine handling repetitive tasks and the student gaining more autonomy. In the same way, many people have said that the home computer will be the death of camaraderie at the office. Once more, we're called upon to choose one or the other, as if these two forms of activity had to be mutually exclusive. Following that argument to its logical conclusion, you might just as well say that masturbation should take the market away from sex.

Many Apple people have one computer at home and one in the office. Contrary to what you might think, this doesn't stop them from going to the office. They like to meet each other, exchange ideas, rub elbows in the cafeteria. They have no desire to work at home exclusively; contrary to what you might think, far from isolating employees from each other, computers create new forms of social relationships. People exchange their tricks, their programs, their information on new models; they communicate through networks.

Some historians bewail the replacement of private letters by the telephone. They complain that people don't write to each other any more and that a great deal of information is therefore lost. Maybe. It is true that people tell each other things on the phone that formerly they would have put in letters. But they can talk much longer and say a lot more. It is true that words exchanged over the phone are not immortal—but our era is not particularly worried about preserving them either. Indeed, we produce far more written words than were ever produced in the past. They're just different, and the historians of the future will be well able to understand them. If you want an instant sociological mirror of something refined by competition, look at advertising or software or paperback books.

I write fewer personal letters than in the days when I went to the Kreisker Boarding School in Saint-Pol-de-Léon and my grandmother used to send me parcels with homemade sausage hidden inside. But personal computers let you send electronic mail: letters, even drawings. They're on the brink of introducing a new form of cultural exchange through networks, thousands of them, in the United States and Europe. Contacts are created between people thousands of miles apart and in different countries. Without these networks, they would never have gotten to "meet" each other.

This debate about solitude is partially linked to another debate that has been going on since the beginning of the Industrial Revolution: the debate about elimination of people's jobs by automation. Since the nineteenth century, workers have feared that machines would take over their jobs. The first important manifestation of this anxiety took place in Nottingham, England, when workers destroyed their steam-powered looms. Today we know that this was a desperate rearguard action and that the new system would eventually take over. The currents of history can devastate countries that fail to make the necessary adjustments at the proper time. France has recently gone through a few ordeals that illustrate the dangers of late adaptation.

I am often asked whether programs like Visicalc mean that accountants aren't needed any longer. Everything depends on what you ask your accountant to do. In my company their job is not simply to keep the books. Accounts are nothing but reports: if you find a management error, this means the error has already been made. But what the accountant can contribute, by financial simulation, is a numerical representation of your hypothesis: "You want to launch this product? Watch out, you'll only sell two thousand." Or: "Your cost price is unrealistic." Or: "You're spending 2.5 percent of the sales volume on telephone bills, and that's twice the industry average." These are complicated calculations that weren't always done in the past. Instead of eliminating jobs, the computer merely performs the mechanical part of the work and leaves people's minds free for other tasks. It does not eliminate the accounting profession; rather, it changes it and makes it more interesting. The computer opens up a wider range of possibilities.

It is true that for the destiny of some companies the computer plays the role of Exterminating Angel. As it reveals flaws, it announces the Apocalypse. The introduction of data processing makes well-managed companies even more competitive, while others crumble under their own weight. This may sound frightening, but in the end it is salutary for the management of a company to face facts. Mistakes must be paid for—there's no getting around it, and a good thing too. I speak from experience, having made many mistakes myself. Errors of judgment about people can burn both parties. But mistakes in market estimates give you back in experience what they cost you in profits, and are far from useless. In a company, the computer works for truth—and there are things that cannot be hidden from it.

7

Marry Them Off!

THE LARGE-SCALE DATA-PROCESSING industry in France has lived through a few misadventures, and despite the fanfare and big plans, it cannot be said to be doing especially well. True, the government has entertained great ambitions for it, even providing, at its birth, a *plan-calcul* (computer plan) designed to pump in the funding needed for it to take off. This is the real problem: cradle-to-grave security. People suddenly realized that the future belonged to data processing, and in France we have some old reflexes that make the government responsible for everyone's future. Money as the protective umbrella—a resurrection of the grand schemes of Colbert, minister of finance to Louis XIV. So they began to coddle data processing enthusiastically, just as Colbert

did the silk-stocking manufacturers. But while Col-[*]
bert's schemes made some sense, because they were
directed at objects, a policy of this nature makes no
sense today. What people don't realize is that now
we are no longer in a hard-goods economy but in a
service economy. This changes everything. In the
tertiary sector the currents of the economy dry up as
soon as you try to centralize them. A computer is not
a thing, like an ashtray or a hat. It is a medium that
dispenses information. Having failed to grasp that
the old schemes were inadequate, the government
had to start again from the top. Just as it did in the
seventeenth century, it imperceptibly changed its role
from referee to player and finally to manufacturer.
With this in mind, we can write another disappoint-
ing chapter—that of French data processing: a series
of broken marriages, chain-reaction mergers, Band-
Aid solutions. A group of companies merges into CII,
but CII cannot succeed all on its own, so it merges
with an American giant. Thus Honeywell-Bull. Because the "giant" wasn't as powerful as people had
hoped, it got back its independence and became Bull
again. When you change names too often, you are
likely to reveal an uncertainty about your identity.

The fact is that everyone is afraid to ask the fundamental question: is it really necessary to have a giant
French data-processing industry? One could very well
argue the contrary, decide that its chronic poor health
condemns it to play supporting roles forever on the

international stage, and close down the factories or
sell them to the Japanese. From the strictly economic
standpoint, these two solutions would be both rational and healthy. Everyone knows that the French
data-processing industry cannot survive without a
good dose of protectionism. What does this mean?
Quite simply that its services are more expensive for
the end consumer. What would happen if we chose
a free-trade solution? Consumers would be allowed
to buy foreign products that are more competitive
and hence cheaper. Their purchasing power would
then be enhanced and they would be able to spend
what was left over as they chose, or put it into savings, which could have only positive effects on the
overall health of the economy. And then, in a sufficiently free market, someone could always be found
to provide the financial fuel for a true invention: it
would encourage innovation, the mother of growth.
Alas, all too often we think of those Frenchmen who
support this point of view as unpatriotic.

So, the patriots ask, don't you think France *has*
to have a national data-processing industry? What
would become of the armed forces without it? We're
surely not going to ask foreigners to manufacture
our military hardware! But what they don't tell us is
that the French armed forces, at this very moment,
are functioning on an American computer made by
Scymour Cray. They also forget that the few French
machines that exist are made largely with compo-

nents imported from Silicon Valley or Japan. It's always very tempting to close off your frontiers; it's so much more comfortable. But what would the data-processing bakers do if they were no longer able to buy their precious flour? The usual argument that it is essential to preserve the French data-processing industry because of vital national interests is nothing but a political lie. Like other sectors of the economy, national defense is international.

Also, you have to imagine what everyday life is like in a nationalized enterprise like Bull, which has a hard time keeping up with its foreign competitors. Bull has competent men and women who ask nothing more than to be allowed to have ideas and make use of their energy, who only want to give the best of themselves to create new, competitive, desirable products. But they also know that, for reasons largely outside their control, this goal is inaccessible in the current situation. They know the dice are loaded: the products they make will be bought, of course, but because they are French, not because they are good. These people are dispossessed of a part of their identity. Their professionalism, their enthusiasm, their love for a job well done—all these qualities are secondary, whereas they should be essential. These people are in the same situation as the rich man who wonders whether people like him for himself or his money. From the fatal moment when he starts asking this question, he can no longer look in the same way at the woman he loves.

We have been told often enough that we absolutely must guarantee the survival of Bull, if only not to increase unemployment. This is probably what is called negative job creation. After repeated mergers and company bailouts, Bull is tottering, even with the support of the government, even in a protected market. The situation is all the more disastrous because there are some outstanding people at Bull—I have hired a few of them. But our little Apple makes four or five times more sales per employee than Bull. And many customers prefer IBM's computers to those of Bull. It is easy to predict that, deprived of French taxpayers' money, Bull would quickly disappear. It is an industrial tool whose existence is artificial and which can no longer claim a place in the world market. We can only hope that the outcome will not be too painful.

The solution of course would be to accept the dramatic but logical conclusion, i.e., pull out altogether. Though rational, it is obviously unrealistic for political and social reasons. Closing Bull would be perceived as a national disgrace, putting twenty thousand people out of work and throwing the country to the powerful IBM lions. But are these reasons really sufficient to justify our continuing to pay taxes for the ridiculous purpose of supporting an industry condemned to make inferior tools? Subsidizing competitive tools is bad enough. But subsidizing noncompetitive tools is worse. Of course, people will reply that Bull computers are better than IBM computers. Maybe they are; it's really a question of personal preference. But it's definitely true that, on a genuinely free market, public and private customers would not buy Bull machines if they were allowed to choose.

One of the "unthinkable" solutions is selling off Bull piecemeal, to—why not?—the Japanese. Heavens! But let's imagine for a moment that Bull ends up with a top-of-the-line machine made by a Japanese company, NEC let's say. Imagine further that the middle level of the market was occupied by a series of machines, also Japanese. We would say that a quiet invasion was underway, as with British Leyland and Honda, Alfa Romeo and Nissan. I'm joking, of course. No one would believe for an instant that that could happen to Bull, with the DPS 8 as the top-of-the-line computer and, more recently, the DPS 7 in the middle.

For Bull to rid itself of its contradictions, it would have to get out from under the protective umbrella beneath which it operates. But no one today can figure out how Bull could escape protectionism. Who are its main customers, after all? Protected markets, that's who: the government, Social Security, the armed forces, the ministries. In short, the spenders of pub-

lic money. A fine state of affairs. When you play golf
you can be protected by a handicap, but you can also
be handicapped. It's a question of phraseology. Protectionism is a double-edged sword that can strike
down those who flourish it. Bull is rather like a cod-
dled child who collapses as soon as he has to con-
front reality on his own.

In any case, this protection is highly relative; let
us not forget that IBM, an American company, has
a firm foothold on French soil and operates factories
that employ twenty-one thousand Frenchmen, providing more jobs than Bull! I would add that, from
the standpoint of Apple, the existence of IBM on the
personal computer market has been very profitable.
First, because it made us come down to earth by putting things in perspective and restoring competition.
Second, because Big Blue lent an air of respectability
to a product that, not so long ago, was considered
marginal and superfluous.

IBM's capital is made in America, it's true, but it
is still a French industry and even patriotic. IBM never
ceases to emphasize this point and is even ready to
enter into agreements with French companies like
Thomson and Telecom and help certain French uni-
versities. If you chase competition away, it comes
galloping back; protectionism is only a frame of mind.
It is predictable that IBM will simultaneously become more and more attractive because of its for-
midable customer-service system and because of its

willingness to become more and more French. I really can't see why Bull couldn't make equally spectacular technological breakthroughs to counterbalance the power of IBM. As I see it, it is certainly not by concentrating on building IBM PC clones that Bull will take off and ensure its independence.

One might wish for a more flexible and dynamic situation. After all, trios are often more entertaining than duets. It would be a real thrill to see French data processing wake up and get moving, if only because it is unhealthy to let IBM take over French industry from the inside, like a Trojan horse. Obviously it would not be in the interests of the French government for IBM to be powerful enough to decide the future of data processing in France. When the day comes that IBM has even more employees and Bull even fewer, and the French government is tempted to protect Bull still further at the expense of IBM, what will IBM's response be? What workers will be left to protect, after all? If France wants to change its tune, though, the dice must be thrown again; we must abstain from direct alliances with IBM, Apple, or the others and try to create a new standard that will encourage Bull to grow until it gains a share of the world market and takes its place beside its competitors. For the moment, these prospects are just pie in the sky. For French data processing to succeed in creating a new and internationally competitive product without resorting to degrading maneuvers like closing down the frontiers, it would have to lock itself up in the laboratory for three or four years and live on a diet of $60 million. It would have to decide to conduct research intensively, to seek ideas the world over, including California, to bring foreign inventors into France, to allow the machines to be made in Taiwan, etc., etc.

In the great patriotic hoopla at the outset, the government had offered a computer plan to French data processing, predicting that high-performance computers would be built. But it had completely forgotten to provide the indispensable complement: a components plan. In other words, the government worried about the boxes but forgot the contents—semiconductors, integrated circuits, chips, etc. Nor was there a VLSI (very-large-scale integrated circuit) plan in France. The present situation is the result of this initial misreading. In fact, there are three technologies of vital importance in the high-technology sector: semiconductors, disk drives, and software. Unfortunately, the only one of these that is up to standard in our country is software: its quality and dynamism are beyond dispute. Why? Because software did not enjoy protectionism. A lucky escape. It seems that the officials of the French Republic tend to lose interest in intangibles and so ignored this essential but almost invisible field. Is this why it's so healthy today?

By the time the government realized the imbalance between the different sectors, it was already late and panic was afoot. To repair the damage we leaped into bed with American companies like National Semiconductor and Harris. These marriages had nothing to do with the identity, culture, or desire of the companies that entered into them; they were merely alliances aimed at catching up in the field of integrated circuits.

The reasoning that followed was, to say the least, paradoxical. If you want to keep a foreign invader away from your shores, marry him! It's an old formula that dates from before the French Revolution. So we began importing knowhow while making products in France. But the children of these unions, which were anything but love matches, today resemble the monsters in a Goya painting—the kind of freaks produced when a decision is made not because it is based on economic sense or meets market needs, but to satisfy the desires of the government.

And yet the World Data Processing and Human Resources Center represents a fine effort. This center, created by Jean-Jacques Servan-Schreiber in 1981 (and since closed), had the legitimate ambition of dealing in competence, not in nationality, and of bringing to France the brightest and best in the computer field. The idea would create a cultural seed that was to impregnate French society with computer science. They called in Seymour Papert, a student of Jean Piaget from M.I.T., and Nicolas Negroponte from Carnegie-Mellon to do research on the child psychology of data processing. The result was a language called Logo, used in schools. With an annual budget of about $21 million expense was no object, so it was possible to buy Digital Equipment computers to do the programming. Some of those in Mitterrand's entourage were aware that France had missed the boat on large-scale data processing, and they tried to get on board when the new-generation data processing came along. But one fine day everything came to a halt, and this noble idea that, under the best conditions, could have led to the creation of French machines, foundered in a sea of political log-rolling. The World Center often bowed to Jean-Jacques Servan-Schreiber. His vision of the future, often clear and correct, was spoiled by deplorable management and, more generally, by deplorable political sense. He himself overpruned the trees he had planted—with the aid of a few politicians who wished him the best, a best that was, however, very French.

A new product can conquer a market only if the joys it affords are greater than the sacrifices entailed by its acquisition. The failure of quadraphonic sound is an excellent example. Stereo-system owners did not feel it worthwhile to replace their entire record libraries to gain just a slight improvement in listening enjoyment. On the other hand, compact disks, which require equipment that also would make an existing record library unplayable, are on the point of taking over because they possess qualities, demonstrable to any consumer, that are superior to those of ordinary LP's. They allow you to listen to music for seventy-four minutes without interruption; they are virtually indestructible; you can skip from one piece to another, from one track to another, by remote control, as often as you like; the sound is clean, with no hiss. Customers want them, and they're worth the sacrifice of replacing an existing record library.

French data processing is ailing because it has neglected these elementary considerations, without which business cannot operate normally. It is ailing because it despised competition. Every night before I go to sleep I say a little prayer for competition. It is because of competition that good machines have been designed: it stimulates inventors, it develops the market. If it did not exist I could not live as I want to, I would have no individual value or yardstick for measuring myself, and I would be lost in the crowd. Or I would be struggling at my job. Let me explain: when I was little, I was told that businessmen were crooks, whereas researchers (a researcher is what I wanted to be) were noble and determined people. I found the truth to be very different. There are far fewer fights among businessmen than among re-

searchers, where there is in-fighting for credit, for
fame, for jobs. Businessmen, as long as they are on
the same team, fight as a team to win the favor of
the market. All CEOs from time to time have a mo-
mentary impulse to eliminate competition. But they
know competition is a necessary condition for fine
automobiles and excellent computers to emerge. If
we want French microcomputers to survive, we must
let them compete on the world market, because the
French market, lively though it is, does have its limits.

Competition is always thought of as a war, a battle *against* other companies. But what if it were a fight
for the favor of the customers? In France there is a
lot of talk about industry, but very little about the
customers who spend their hard-earned money on
the products of industry. I'm talking about customers, not consumers. There are products that cannot
be "consumed." We consume milk or bread and, once
they're consumed, they disappear. We don't consume a book, a house, a computer, or a record. And
in France when we talk about consumers we always
feel obliged to speak of them in a protective tone of
voice as if "those people" were not capable of managing by themselves. But we are all consumers, and
it would be a great mistake to underestimate us: we
won't buy an inferior product for long. In fact, what
we forget is that consumers are workers first and
foremost. We all know that workers at General Motors check the serial number of a car they are think-

ing of buying to make sure it wasn't made in a period of absenteeism or when everyone had a hangover—one of those famous "Monday cars." But in France, when we're called upon to do something really useful, like a comparative test on tires—common in the United States—the goodwill evaporates. On the one hand, paternalistic speeches are made, and on the other, tests that could save lives are discouraged.

One day I read in the columns of a consumer magazine a letter from a customer who said he was dissatisfied with his Apple *III*. I immediately wrote him: "If there is a manufacturing defect we will replace your machine at once and would be happy to send you a small gift to say we're sorry, etc." At the same time, I wrote to the magazine to ask that any other complaints be referred to me. But it took the publisher three months to send on my letter to the customer! Here is a magazine that insists on manufacturers having a responsive customer service, and it takes three months to forward a letter!

Competition (and I am not the first to say this) is not anarchy. The American model is interesting precisely because the government, by its antitrust legislation, protects competition by preventing huge companies from forming and then controlling the market. The American government does not take lightly its role as referee, and on this important point the free-trade myth needs to be toned down. John Sculley, CEO and chairman of the board of Apple,

once told me that he can't telephone John Young,
CEO of Hewlett-Packard, without taking all sorts of
precautions. And there are certain subjects—prices,
distribution, etc.—that they are strictly forbidden to
talk about under any circumstances, whether on the
phone or by their private swimming pools. If it can
be proved, by the length of telephone calls for example, that two industrialists making competitive
products have had repeated conversations, they may
get taken to court. The laws are so strict on this point
that they border on being unconstitutional: it is up
to the accused to prove his innocence. If it is discovered, for example, that the prices of their two companies went up or down at the same time, and if it
is found that they talked on the phone during this
period, they are presumed guilty and risk penalties
as severe as imprisonment. It goes without saying that
the other executives in these companies are also under strict surveillance. So the Referee State does not
get involved in the choice of customers; it confines
itself to setting up the rules of the game to prevent
abuses. But this is a task it takes seriously. It's a little
bit like basketball: you're not allowed to hold on to
the ball and run with it, *and* if you have an advantage, your opponents can take it away from you. It's
a wonderful game precisely because you can be ahead
one minute and behind the next. What is so interesting about the United States is that nothing can be
held on to for good. There is always a risk, and you

always have to prove yourself. On the other hand, the range of possibilities is always open. Make a fortune, change jobs, start out again from the bottom . . . these are events that are part of the natural course of life.

In France, they hold on to the ball for too long. It's not only the government that is to blame. For one thing, like Normandy farmers, we are surrounded by hedges and ditches. As soon as a sector is set up, people try to protect it, erect barriers, make exclusivity conditions. The race is to the privileged, blocking the free flow of changing desires and stifling invention, imagination, fantasy. There is a fixed number of pharmacists, the Medical Association, the fixed price paid for a notarial office, government personnel regulations, National Savings Bank regulations specifying that hiring must be done from inside except for entry-level jobs, and so on. What the French fear above all else is having to change when they think they have it made: they want to have their cake and eat it too. These exclusivity restrictions, found in every field of endeavor, have really done what the free-economy people have been accused of doing: they have allowed a few to rake in profits at the expense of the many. To justify the fixed number of pharmacists and limit the number of dispensaries, it takes years to become a pharmacist—longer than to go through engineering school. Is it really necessary to study all that time to know that a certain two drugs must not be given at the same time? Wouldn't it be enough to indicate incompatibilities by package labeling? We're stifling under the weight of economic feudalism.

In 1981 the French microcomputer train whistled, pulled into the station, slowed down, stopped, whistled to announce its departure, started again slowly, and left. French industry watched it go without reacting. This story is all the more devastating because the microcomputer was invented by . . . a Frenchman. His name was André Truong Thi and he managed a company called REE (Recherches et Études Électroniques), located right opposite Hewlett-Packard in the Courtaboeuf industrial zone. In the early seventies, well before Jobs, Wozniak, and the others, he had the idea of putting a microprocessor inside a computer. He had the right idea but was unable to make it bear fruit; he made the fatal mistake of relentlessly striving to endow his invention with the attributes and functions of larger machines. He wanted his micro to be a shrunken mini—smaller, cheaper, but in the same league with large computers—instead of making something altogether different. His other error was to orient software design toward accounting applications instead of creating innovative intellectual tools. What is more, he failed to take a serious look at quality, cost, and sales. But he had a very active public-relations department. There was a lot of flag-waving, and an agreement was made with the American company Warner-Swasey to allow REE to set up on the American market. All of twenty machines must have been sold! This lamentable affair was one of the many contracts signed in this century that were somewhat shameful window dressing to conceal some rather seamy industrial and commercial realities.

The destiny of a manufacturer is not necessarily tied to his size in the world market. This is well illustrated by the automobile industry. A few years ago, the conventional wisdom was that you needed to produce three million cars per year to be viable. Mercedes, BMW, and Volvo, for example, as well as Jaguar after privatization, proved the contrary with 100,000 to 150,000 cars per year. Of course these are expensive, highly esteemed vehicles. The market is filled with examples showing that the perception of the value of a product counts for more than the producer's size.

Finally, after the train pulled out of the station, Frenchmen took a somewhat belated plunge into microcomputers. Today, as I said earlier, if the industry is to get out from under, it will have to spend the time and resources to get technologically ahead and one fine day come up with a sufficiently high-performance product to find a niche in the world market. I'm very hard-nosed about this: there is no other solution—besides putting a fence around France and making all-French machines that Frenchmen will buy because they have no other choice.

8

The Proof of the Pudding

"DO YOU WANT TO GO ON selling sugared water to kids, or do you want to change the world?" By asking this question, Steve Jobs persuaded John Sculley, former president of Pepsi-Cola, to take over the management of Apple Computers. It was usually very difficult to resist the devilish charm of our departed *Líder Maximo*. What is more, the phenomenal rate at which the company he created spread across the market does indeed prove that his activities have changed something in the world. Things happen so quickly when you work at Apple that you sometimes feel like the poor donkey in the La Fontaine fable who carried relics and naïvely imagined that the wonderful incense odor filling his nostrils was intended for him personally.

At Apple France, everyone sits in front of a machine and not behind it. The machine is the mirror of ideas. Both the executive and the secretary are doing more or less the same thing; for example, they are trying to serve the dealers so well and so fast that the dealers can't do without us. When someone comes by to offer me a service, I usually put my cards right on the table in a way that startles some people. I ritually ask, "What's this thing of yours going to do for me?" Those who don't understand this kind of language get angry, irritated by such a lack of delicacy, and that's the end of it. But most people catch on very fast. They recover from their initial surprise, burst out laughing, and begin to explain: "Here's what it'll do for you. Soon you won't be able to do without me. . . . Of course, if there's nothing in it for you, we might as well say so long."

In fact, if the people around me don't bring me new ideas, I get very unhappy. I choose them, but they choose me too; in no sense is it a one-way relationship. Once they've come on board, they all find their niches. We are aware that not everyone has the same set of intellectual tools and feelings, and that a particular talent isn't always revealed right away. There are those who know how to get information, and those who are past masters in the art of processing or presenting it; others can answer requests for information and reassure the discontented; still others have an intuition for what obstacles lie ahead.

The division of labor evolves on the spot, day after day, in a process of compromise that changes according to structural needs and the need for flexibility. Let me repeat that the growth rate in our market, even when "slowed down" to 30 or 40 percent, facilitates change. We are relaxed because we can always find a job elsewhere if necessary. Financial security helps us to look on the bright side of things; of that I am very well aware.

Apple France was legally established in May 1981. We sent out our first shipment on January 4, 1982. We got together, and together we succeeded in exploiting luck and converting certain obstacles into advantages. Here is one example. We were a tiny company and we were afraid of being flooded by the volume of business. After close consideration and a great deal of hesitation, we finally made a decision to keep things simple: the prices of our computers would be the same, whatever the quantity ordered. This step was contrary to all the usual laws of the marketplace, but the decision, inspired by circumstance, freed us in our relationship with our dealers to spend our time helping them to sell to the real customers. (Our customers have, in a sense, our money in their pockets, money we want to get into *our* pockets through those of our dealers.) The dealers' discount is always the same and they know that this aspect of the relationship is not negotiable. As soon as they have realized this they stop fidgeting and it's no longer necessary to renegotiate. This very simple decision was a great help to us and, what is more, stopped the great birds of prey from snatching the growing market.

If a huge chain could buy Apples at a 45 percent discount while Jean-Louis Orsini, a relatively small dealer in Boulogne-Billancourt, got only 30 percent, Orsini would be unjustly penalized. Jean-Louis Orsini was the first dealer I visited, incognito, after I signed my contract with Tom Lawrence. When I went to see him, I was still officially the president of Exxon Office Systems, France. We chatted for a while and I asked whether he had heard that Apple was thinking about opening a headquarters in Paris. What did he think? He was enthusiastic; he knew about the project already. "They'll be setting up in Neuilly. You should go work for them; they're great." I was all the happier about his reaction because I had already signed my contract. Nothing is pleasanter than to have someone confirm you've made a good deal. Orsini is an excellent specialized dealer. He'll never have fifteen thousand square feet of floor space—that's not his ambition—but he is highly competent in what he does. If we had had differential pricing practices, we would never have been able in a growing and expanding market to give people like him the chance to put their talent to work. We would only have been able to work with those who had both talent *and* money, which would have been a pity.

Many companies explained to me that it was essential to give them higher discounts because of the inventory costs that they had to pass on to their customers. We responded by paring delivery times down to the bone, sometimes to less than twenty-four hours; this took care of their storage problems. Some of them asked us to widen their profit margin just because they were big and fat—a line of reasoning that will never cease to astonish me. So we stood firm. I still don't understand why no one else uses standard discounts. Of course, I am aware that we can't continue this way when the market matures, i.e., when the supply is greater than the demand, as in the case of automobiles, for example.

It is also true that to put over a policy like ours you have to have a good product: "Thanks for sales and marketing, but dear God give us some products," says my old buddy Barry Ross, a former Brooklyn branch manager for Exxon who was rocketed into the position of vice-president for Europe in Geneva. When the two of us started working together, we glared at each other like cat and dog, but we quickly realized that we were born to understand each other. I'll never forget some of the ludicrous situations we went through together. He had the bewildered air of the New York Jew who, on his first trip to Europe, found himself in a restaurant in Lyons where they served him tripe and pigs' feet without warning. Nor will I forget his hilarious face when he asked for the men's room and was given a bone, marrow and all, from which dangled a key on a string. The key opened a door into the old-fashioned type of Turkish toilet, which consists of a hole in the floor with pieces of newspaper hanging from a nail.

It sometimes happens that manufacturers try to sell a bad product. When they notice it's not moving, they often try to blame the customers for their problem, saying they're Neanderthals incapable of appreciating an excellent product. But there *are* bad products; we know that only too well. In our company there was the case of the Apple *III*, which was suddenly launched on the market; many machines were defective, and we had to replace fourteen thousand of them. I must say that, as far as enhancing our reputation, this operation was a success. We received thank-you letters telling us that General Motors would never have done the same. But in the case of the Apple *III* there were other mistakes. We had artificially decided that it would be a professional machine, which meant that the Apple II was unsuitable for high-level work. We even gave the Apple *III* a hard disk with what was at that time a large capacity, and in order to protect the *III* we decided not to do the same thing for the Apple II. As if that were not enough, we made programmers' lives difficult by giving them very little information on the programming of the Apple *III*, although they were on top of everything for the Apple II. So there weren't enough programs and the scent of infinity never wafted out when buyers opened the box. Later with the Lisa we made similar mistakes; this machine was too expensive and too difficult to program, and we had chosen an elitist distributor network for it, while what people wanted from us were personal computers. A single error is not enough to capsize a good product, but the memory of the Apple *III* enabled us to react faster. The market had voted. Exit the Apple *III*, which its users, connoisseurs all, nonetheless consider a machine of choice, but a choice we had made too difficult. We made the Lisa compatible with the best-selling Macintosh and brought down its price. The scent of infinity wafted back. We even changed the name to Macintosh XL (Extra-Large or Ex-Lisa). Sales went back up. Still, we had to abandon it without honor or glory since we failed to raise sales to an adequate profit margin at a time when market growth was slowing down. All of which proves that it is difficult to revive a product that has made a poor start. Other companies, larger ones, have had the same experience. The market is discerning—the proof of the pudding is in the eating.

When I'm at a meeting of young executives I'm always astonished to find that their ideas are so antiquated. They in turn must think I'm eccentric, provocative, even irresponsible. I tell them for example that each Apple France employee has two machines, one at home and another at the office. Or that we have no more than four hierarchical levels because we do everything we can to stay lean and on our toes. On the other hand, our salary policy has no upper limit; it's the job market that decides. The executives to whom I tell this story are a little flummoxed; they tell me they couldn't do that, and they're probably right. If we pay high salaries it's because there are relatively only a few of us and the payroll is a very small percentage of our sales figures.

It's also because we're sailing before the wind. Like everywhere else, it happens sometimes that customers call us to complain that their Apple II or Macintosh is playing tricks on them. When I ask them to send it back so I can reimburse them, they lose their tempers: "That's not what I want at all!" All they're asking me for is a little help, some advice, or a repair. They can't imagine being without their machines; rather than send them back, customers would willingly endure the machines' occasional tricks. Thus it is that a conflict becomes an anecdote. I feel privileged, after all, to find myself in a situation where circumstances compel me to do what I want to do anyway.

Like putting talented people to work. In 1981, in California, someone told me one day: "There are two rather strange Frenchmen inventing things in a lab in Cupertino; you should go see them." I went right away, and found myself in the presence of two very busy, bearded, long-haired individuals who had taken an Apple II apart and strewn its innards over the table. There were wires and oscilloscopes everywhere—an incredible mess. They were developing boards to improve the graphics on Apple II+. And these boards had the inestimable advantage of being able to connect directly to one of the great French inventions of recent years: the Peritel connector, which made it possible to plug directly into the electronics of the cathode-ray tube and control the reds, greens, and yellows in the picture. Before the Peritel connector, you had to install, behind the computer, a system emitting signals that fed into the antenna and then had to be demodulated. It was an expensive method, and it reduced the quality of the picture. So the two rather strange Frenchmen, Philippe Chaillat and Didier Chaligné, still as hairy and enthusiastic as Dr. Bronson in the comic strip *Alley Oop*, came to see me in Paris. I told them: "You're going to set up your own company; we'll help you, and we'll distribute your invention." I suddenly wanted to make them business partners and not employees. I was convinced that this independence would stimulate them into making future inventions. Initially they hesitated, they didn't want to "go into business," they wanted to stay quietly in their corner and tinker with their machines without bothering about anything else. But they were quite happy to be convinced. They called their company "Le Chat Mauve" (The Purple Cat) and made several hundred thousand dollars in sales with us. Then when the Apple II C came out, they manufactured a circuit in the United States that hooks up behind the machine and creates beautiful color pictures. One of them even made the trip to California with his leg in a plaster cast. They now have a subcontractor, production is getting started, and they take care of component purchasing. They work with us and not for us, and that makes all the difference. This kind of alliance enchants me and gives an extra meaning to my job.

And I don't have to wear a gray flannel suit. When you see how French businessmen still feel obliged to dress, you sense you're looking at nineteenth-century foundry owners. The color of the suit also reflects the ethics of the man who wears it. Big industry represents institutional might par excellence, by contrast with personal power. It shows itself in its true colors, through the gray of the suit: a Moloch, a Leviathan, a universe of corporations and conglomerates, in which faces, individual features, and differences are erased. In Silicon Valley it would be quite difficult to create a scandal with one's clothes. People dress more or less anyhow. There is no uniform, except for the salesmen, whom you can sometimes recognize by their somewhat too-well-pressed suits. At Apple it's impossible to guess correctly who is the boss by the absence or presence of a tie. People change the way they dress from one day to the next. You find someone you remember covered with hair has turned into a well-scrubbed preppy, or bump into financial types who have suddenly taken to walking around all week wearing the same T-shirt with a couple of holes in it.

This irreverence sometimes finds its way into our advertising. When the Macintosh came out we even took out a big ad in the French Communist newspaper *l'Humanité* that said: "The time has come for a capitalist to make a revolution." At the time I had made a proposal that could have extricated the French press from its difficulties: because of the capabilities offered by the big computers, I suggested streamlining the production of *Le Figaro* (a conservative newspaper) and *l'Humanité*. The project would keep just one of the editorial staffs, that of *l'Humanité*, the more professional one, which would produce its newspaper as usual. Then the computers would take care of reversing the negative or positive proposals of each article to obtain a text that would read exactly the opposite and you'd get the contents of *Le Figaro* at no extra cost. An elegant, practical, economical solution that would have done honor to French genius. I'm still wondering why they didn't take me up on the idea. . . .

It was through one of these advertisements that I met Étienne Roda-Gil: *Don't tell my mother I'm working at Apple, she thinks I'm at IBM. . . . If you're capable of programming the Song of Solomon into a 68000 Assembler and selling American computers to the French Internal Revenue Service or writing product brochures like Étienne Roda-Gil. . . .* I fell in love with this son of a Spanish anarchist worker in 1973 through a Julien Clerc record he'd written the lyrics for. It was the heyday of that devilish pair. His esoteric poetry sold millions of copies. To sell, says an erroneous piece of folk wisdom, you have to appeal to the lowest common denominator. This does not apply in the case of Roda-Gil, who wrote the songs of Mort Schumann and Angelo Branduardi. It is because of this admiration that I used his name, though we had never met. Evidently someone told him that Apple was using his name in its advertising, and he came to see us, curious to find out what was going on. As soon as he entered our offices, with their paneled walls, he felt at home; he liked the atmosphere. "I understand, you are the Abbey of Thélème," he said. "You are waging the battle of 'knowledge is fun' against the dusty academics" (a reference to Rabelais). He had that instant and correct vision characteristic of poets. He immediately came up with an idea: "If I did a television piece on computers and children, I would write a little rhyme that would start: "C'est un professeur, il est bien, c'est un professeur, il ne sait rien," which one might translate: "Teacher, Teacher, what a hero, Teacher, Teacher—don't know zero!" Étienne Roda-Gil is a modest man; his songs are better known than he is himself. One day when I was talking to him about "Poisson mort" over a meal at the Boudin Sauvage he told me that Pierre Richard had once suddenly appeared beside him in a Paris restaurant, knelt down on the floor, recited "Poisson mort," shook his hand, and returned to his table to eat. I felt less lonely.

Étienne Roda-Gil is one of those poets who have what's called a style, which means that those who love his poems always recognize them. One day I was reading an article in *l'Express* on Angelo Branduardi that quoted some lines of a song which told a story of a balloon and a child, and I guessed correctly that these lines were by Roda-Gil. He is one of those people who have turned up in my life at the most unexpected moments and opened up new horizons each time. I'm glad I'm working for Apple; after all, it's the company that published a poem by Ray Bradbury.

The image we put across is faithful to what we are, to what we sell, to our way of working. In France, the importance of the brand image is still poorly understood; it is taken for window dressing or fakery. Perhaps this is a form of modesty, linked to our complicated relationship with success and money. In fact, marketing is an essential part of business. It's not enough to have a good product; you have to know how to sell it, which means making it known and making it desirable. A "good image" is an image that whets desire. What is a washing machine for? For freeing you to do something besides watching the laundry while it goes around. But not just anything. A few years ago an ad for a washing machine showed a housewife sitting in an armchair, blissfully munching chocolate while her machine was doing the work. Big mistake: no mother, even if she adores chocolate, wants to think that this greedy passion is the only activity in her life. It would probably have been better to show her reading, visiting a museum, or looking after her family. On the other hand, an ad that showed a child beside his mother, starting the washing machine, gave a flattering image of the product and of the user.

There's no harm in pleasing. In today's economic system, enticement is a reality that determines many other realities. The makers of an American brand of instant coffee were worrying about their sales. They ran some consumer tests that showed coffee drinkers were unable to distinguish between instant and real coffee. Yet the real coffee was selling better. The marketing department was seething: our product isn't selling even though, by objective standards, it's good! So it organized some surveys. Two groups of housewives representative of a certain population were given identical shopping lists and asked to draw a portrait of the woman who had written them. There was only one difference between the lists—the coffee. So the investigators could be certain that the differences in the portraits would be due to the type of coffee chosen. Result: the housewife who bought regular coffee was described as a maternal woman who cared about her family's well-being. The buyer of instant coffee was thought to have a tendency to neglect her maternal role and to skimp on her household tasks. So instant coffee was selling poorly because women wanted a good image of themselves—that of a good wife and mother. It is high time businessmen realized that the economy is a domain governed by emotions, desires. Economists spend their time being wrong and contradicting one another not just because the phenomena are complex and the data insufficient, but also because they are obsessed by the idea that all these phenomena are rational and that one day they'll discover the laws responsible. Maybe they will, but if they're going to get there they'll have to reflect on the emotions that link us to the objects we live with every day.

In 1984 we decided to change our working environment. The inside dividing walls of the Apple France building were removed and then, after a few transitional months living out of packing cases, we were working in a huge area that look like an American-style newsroom. Business was done in noise and hustle, not in silence and meditation. A communications company can only function if communication is also going on inside its walls and departments. We worked with one another as a team, and our identity as a service enterprise was at stake in this choice—our identity as sellers of flexible, user-friendly, Californian machines.

The customers are not unhappy that these machines come from California; they have the myth in their heads, and they have the feeling of participating in a more laid-back life-style. When people who call us are put on hold, they listen to the delicious voice of Chris Graffiti tell them extraordinary tales about the famous "Pear Computer Company" or Californian massage. A way of loosening up the atmosphere while passing on our ideas. Most people are charmed, and some even ask to be put back on hold to hear the rest. Only one customer thus far has complained of this "lack of seriousness." We probably don't think of seriousness in the same way he does. For us, what is serious is the quality of the product and management, the pleasure of a job well done. And . . . just pleasure for its own sake. Basically, we are convinced that marketing and distribution are essential values, because the economy is not (as is too often believed) just a marketplace where goods and money change hands, but a limitless space in which desires can wander freely.

How did Steve Jobs, that handsome and tragic character out of some novel, that visionary monster, aesthete, lonely, detestable and fascinating creature, manage to bring it off? Once he asked me how to keep his hair from falling out. I answered that the only solution is to keep it inside. Which he did. He had just turned thirty. He is one of the heroes of this civilization of wunderkinder who found their own businesses. At age nineteen, it was he who begged his friend Wozniak, who must have been two or three years older, to agree to establish a company.

I am lucky to work with people I like, not with stereotypes. At age forty-three, it is not necessary to be pot-bellied, with an ulcer and hypertension, and be getting over three divorces in order to be a good boss. Nor is it necessary, like Steve Jobs, to be handsomer than Robert Redford and as appealing as the Pied Piper. What is important is to have the ability to transmit ideas. It would be wrong to say that the physical charm of Jobs had no influence on the destiny of the firm he created and then left. It would be just as wrong to say that all he did was entice. He and John Sculley, who is as virtuous and old-fashioned as Jobs is sensual and modern but just as dazzling in his own way, are men convinced of the power of ideas. They are people who have consideration for others, but don't let their own toes get stepped on. They are capable of being firm without brutality, of talking a lot but also listening. They have an air of integrity, meaning that they are fully themselves but don't ask others to be like them. They are people whom I admire and envy, people who have made me a better person.

I admire people who succeed, whether they are pot-bellied and full of Alka-Seltzer or athletic and graceful. I am always annoyed when I hear certain people demean those who have succeeded. They wisecrack as best they can: "How can he succeed when he's so stupid? How can such an ugly man have such a beautiful wife?" I can't help it, even when I meet a man who looks like nobody in particular but who has established a going concern—I can't help thinking that he can't be as insignificant as he looks; he has found his path, he must have special talent.

Life is an enormous Brownian motion of encounters. There are those whose eyes are open, who see the signals made to them and answer. Others wear blinders that stop them from seeing and grabbing opportunities. You have to be awake when opportunity knocks. Except in extreme circumstances, I am convinced that everyone has the power of helping to determine the essentials of his life's path.

This certainty sustains me in the ups and downs of daily life and helps me answer the questions I sometimes ask about my actions. Nobody's perfect . . . I know I annoy some people. I can't resist the temptation to make wisecracks; I have a tendency to play pranks that may be irritating. I am sure that, in the course of my career, I have hurt people. Sometimes I fear that I am too comfortably settled into the system, too assimilated, at risk of losing contact with reality. On occasion, I am not even sure of resisting the temptation to exhibit a little cowardice. What would happen if a future president were to take umbrage at my criticisms of the government? Would I have the courage to stick to my guns if I met him? What concessions, what compromises would I be forced to make? I don't know. What I do know is that the path I have taken rarely leads me into such situations. Unlike politicians, I am never placed in the position of outright lying. I'm sorry for them; they must suffer. In a way, I'm glad they're doing the dirty work instead of me.

9

To Suffer With

TWO FRIENDS MEET IN THE STREET. Pete's wearing a new suit, and Joe takes a fancy to it. After a little persuasion, Pete ends up giving his tailor's address to his friend. Joe goes to see him that very day, and the tailor welcomes him with every courtesy. A new suit? Of course, sir. That'll be $1,000. Joe nearly falls over backward. $1,000 for a new suit! But the tailor explains: "You have to understand that we don't do things by halves here. First of all we'll send an artistic consultant to immerse himself in your professional and home environment so that the cut will be tailored to your personality. Then we'll send a technical adviser out to Australia to pick out a sheep. We'll send the wool to Scotland where they have the best spinners. The thread'll go to Manchester where they do the best dyeing. Then the suit will be made in Ireland. Finally, after five fittings, you'll have a totally unique suit." Joe, impressed, agrees that $1,000 is a pretty good price for all that. But he's still worried: he needs his suit next week. "Don't worry," says the tailor, "you'll have it!"

There are two lies in the computer business. The first is the tailor's lie—you'll have it tomorrow. It's the answer engineers routinely give when asked when their programs will be ready. When I hear this sentence I know I have to get a grip on myself. Software writing is still essentially a young art, a kind of craftsmanship. Some projects can get one or two years behind, or may be dropped altogether. The reason is simple: you can't put a lot of people onto writing a program, or you'd spend more time coordinating them than getting the job done. Everyone knows that adding personnel to a late project will definitely delay it even further. First of all you have to bring the newcomers up to speed, and the only people to do the teaching are those already laboring on the project. So the delay just gets longer and longer. What's more, one extra person added to the coordination puzzle is likely to complicate things at every level, both organizational and interpersonal. The fascinating thing about all this is that by the time you find out a project is overdue, it's already too late to do anything about it. Piling on the pressure won't do any good. Nothing remains but wheedling, threats, and pleas. You can also resign yourself to accepting less satisfactory performance, or put an entirely new team on the job in the hope that the new guys will be better and that you can cut your time losses.

The second lie is even more widespread. It can be expressed in two words, which are both a slogan and a myth: "It's compatible." Why do manufacturers insist on not being compatible with one another? And why is any particular manufacturer not really compatible with himself? Before going into detail on this subject, let's make a visit to our ancestors, the ancient Romans. Compatible comes from two Latin words: *cum*, with, and *patire*, to suffer. To suffer with. An irony of etymology.

The first question is that of the universal, unique standard. It would be great if you could go from one machine to another with your diskette the way you go from one stereo to another with your LP or your compact disk. Ah, but this would mean that the industry was mature and all that was needed was to improve a stable technology. Stability would have become more important than the potential advantages of novelty. But our industry is still young and rich in unexplored technologies, preventing us from casting in bronze a standard that would last several decades, like the LP record.

Conversely, it would be absurd to have a different type of program for every type of machine. This would force programmers to write two or three hundred versions of Multiplan—too many to be economically viable. Caught between the thrust of technological innovation and the need to spread high development and software investments over a large number of computers, the industry is gravitating toward a compromise: a limited number of standards.

But even within a single standard things get complicated. This brings us to the second question—compatibility within a single standard. Here we are faced with a dual problem: the ambitions of the engineers and the evolution of technology. When a new machine using a particular standard first sees the light of day, you never know whether the changes were due to a noble desire on the engineers' part to let the world benefit from advances in technology or whether they were just driven by a passion to accomplish something new.

Still, the novelty thus introduced into the overall structure means that compatibility is no longer absolute. This is true for all manufacturers, to the point that a company like Compaq can claim that it is more IBM-compatible than IBM itself, without surprising anyone in the business.

The secret of success in the delicate area of compatibility with oneself lies in the degree of incompatibility that the new model introduces. If a large enough number of programs are compatible, the marketplace will follow with new versions, fairly easy to develop because the innards of the machine do not change too much. So the software library can move more or less smoothly from one machine to another. If the improvements find favor, even if they create minor incompatibilities, so much the better.

One might hope, in a universe of absolutes, yes or no, that there would be a simpler answer to the question of compatibility. You sometimes wonder whether there is a little devil somewhere to whom we secretly pay homage because he creates confusion that keeps us busy and makes us indispensable.

In the case of a true technological breakthrough rather than a minor improvement, incompatibility is necessary. This is true when it comes to the creation of a new standard, a family of machines, a dynasty. Why is Macintosh not compatible with the Apple II? Because its designers wanted to create something radically different: a machine that talked in pictures rather than text, that can perceive a movement of the hand, and whose standard should last ten years.

Creation of a standard is no small matter. Software writers only want to work if they believe their efforts will be published. So they choose the standard they think will win out. But the standard will only win if good programmers write for it. You need the chicken and the egg at the same time. It's something like Hollywood. Say I want Paul Newman for my next film but I also need $12 million. Where do I start? You have to go see the programmers and tell them, "I have this extraordinary machine. You'll see. It's difficult to program but it'll take off like a rocket, and we'll be there to help you." And then, because of the programmers, it really does become extraordinary and realizes its potential.

Programmers are the artists of technology. This is why I do the job I do: I like artists *and* technology. For a computer to realize its internal promise, you have to convince the good programmers of its merits. Remember, though: when they're working on a new standard, programmers have to adapt to new working tools. It's as if a novelist, every time he wrote a new book, had to go from engraving on stone to papyrus to the goose quill to a nylon tip.

Technology evolves constantly, with the occasional breakthrough. These breakthroughs imply risks, renunciations, transpositions. Rewriting an existing program for a new standard is a bit like arranging a piano score for the organ, or even the violin. A new library must be compiled for each new standard.

The condor is a creature that flies at top energy efficiency. Man, on foot, is on the bottom rung of the efficiency ladder. But as soon as he gets on a bicycle his performance exceeds that of the condor. The computer is the bicycle of the mind. In 1980 Apple launched the advertising slogan "Wheels for the mind." It would have been even more correct to say "Wings for the mind." The computer is an instrument that allows the mind to take flight. What counts is for progress in technology to give priority to compatibility with the desires of human beings, with their intelligence, and not compatibility with other machines.

10

In the Labyrinth

VIEWED UNDER THE MICROSCOPE, a computer chip, a tiny piece of silicon, looks like an aerial photograph of the Grand Canyon. Gullies, hills, rocky paths winding in every direction, cliffs, rocks, slopes. . . . It's a superb vision that makes you feel you're *reading the mind* of its creator: the paths he took, the obstacles he surmounted, the steps backward, the hesitations. The logic is inscribed in the material and science shows the beauty of its forms. A chip is a work of art stamped out by the millions and found on the street, in daily life, in cars, credit cards, handheld calculators. We are living in an era when an object no longer has to be one of a kind to be a work of art.

It all started when the ambiguous properties of semiconductors were discovered—those materials that, unlike copper (which conducts electricity in all directions), conduct in one direction only. They are called semiconductors because they are neither good conductors like metals (gold or copper) nor insulators like glass. What's really fascinating is that semiconductors pass current only because of the impurities they contain. The discovery of the need to add an impurity (specialists speak of "doping") led electronic engineers to the heart of the matter: solid-state physics.

Information is essentially based on finding out about the insides of crystals, the chain of labyrinths created through increasingly refined optics and mechanics, by an ever-more-delicate touch in implanting the right foreign body in the right spot. For semiconductors it all began with the crystal set: a whisker resting on an iron sulfide crystal allows the current to flow in one direction only. When this happens, the high-frequency alternating current carrier disappears, leaving the Bach prelude that modulates (creates variations in) the carrier. I can still hear music in the headphones of my childhood. The difficulty is to find the point of contact between the whisker and the crystal that produces a loud, stable signal.

This effect was known with materials other than iron sulfide. Research into the best materials that exhibited this property showed that it was common to certain crystalline structures and that excessive purity spoiled everything.

From the whisker on the crystal we went on to a small capsule containing a germanium crystal and a whisker attached at the factory, then a whisker with junctions, boundaries between two materials. Still one-directional. A little later an engineer, Shockley, discovered how to add a third electrode, a third wire; henceforth it become possible to influence the current passing between the first two conductors at will: modulate it, control it, amplify it. One thing led to another. From the simple whisker and crystal, we have advanced to integrated circuits containing transistors, resistors, capacitors, and, most important, several silicon chips that organize the traffic flow throughout. Electrodes that open and close serve as passageways and gates between the semiconductors.

A certain Ted Hoff had the idea of transforming a custom integrated circuit for a manufacturer of Japanese handheld calculators into a generic product offered to everyone. The microprocessor was born at Intel. It immediately whetted the desire of its creators. There was a seed in that tiny silicon chip that would sprout into tens of billions of dollars for the personal computer industry. Devotees had always wanted their own computers, and Ted Hoff was to give them the chance to realize their dream.

A circuit is a route, a set of paths, with links; a

network of roads. A computer is a labyrinth. Inside the case, thousands of gates open and close and connect with one another in a series of ultrafast operations. When one gate is opened it may cause another gate further on to open or close. The computer has a feedback capacity that enables it to change its own actions as a function of the results of these actions. An elementary example is the flush toilet: the water level in the tank rises and pushes up the lever attached to the float. At a certain point the valve closes. Elementary feedback. This could be made more complicated. Imagine that, at a certain level, the lever flushed the toilet instead of closing the water inlet: you'd get an effect that the experts call "relaxation oscillations." The beauty of the computer is its ability to run a complex, variable program. It is quite different from a uniform sequence of operations, like the sequential mechanical "programmer" of a washing machine. What the computer plays is a feedback game in all its complexity and inversions.

There is a very good explanation of the beauties of feedback inversion. An old Arabian sheik calls his two sons to his bedside and says something like this to them: "I'm going to die soon and one of you will inherit my kingdom—the one who wins the race . . . of slowness. You'll race on horseback to the other end of the kingdom, and the owner of the horse that passes the frontier last will be my successor." The ministers were panic-stricken: how long would such a race last? Forever? But after a few hours the two brothers were seen galloping out of the gates of the city at full speed. What had happened? They had switched horses, and the slow race had become a fast race.

Let's go back to the flush toilet and imagine for a moment that the link between the rising float and the valve is "dependent." In other words, imagine that the opening or closing of the valve is no longer strictly a function of the height of the water or the position of a rod, but that the effects produced by the rising water depend on the status of other flush-toilet mechanisms which are themselves dependent, and so on. This suggests the kind of intellectual labyrinth to be found inside a computer. To describe the functioning of a programmable computer, Alan Turing, one of the founding geniuses of computer science, proposed a minimalist model. A strip of paper of infinite length divided into small squares passes in front of a window the same size as the squares of paper. The program consists of deciding what action will ensue as a function of what appears in front of the window: writing zero or one, making the strip of paper move rightward or leftward. The beauty of this simple model is that, in theory, it contains the basic structure of all the computers in the world.

Thus far we have talked only about the hardware. But in fact the software is different only in appearance: the structure of the machine describes

THE THIRD APPLE

the "mechanical" sequence of the openings and clos-
ings of gates. The software is supposed to manipulate this sequence. The program causes the machine
to pass through a certain number of states; then there
is a final state, a result. In fact, the hardware and
software, to use Marvin Minsky's image, are only two
different levels of crystallization of the same type of
structure, of information. This is indeed true—to the
extent that computers have a hierarchy of programming levels.

I program in Basic. In reality, I prepare data for
another program called the interpreter, which will
execute the instructions I have written in *my* Basic
program. This interpreter will itself call on a software layer often referred to as the system. It sends
calls to the system, which acts like a microfiche reader
or the writing on a screen. This same system manipulates, either directly or through one or two other
layers, the hardware, the microprocessor, the mem-
ory, and the input|output units. What do you call
software frozen in hardware? *Firmware*, of course! But
if we stop to worry about the actual boundary between the hardware and the software, we won't reach
any very practical conclusions.

The role of personal computers is precisely to
open this universe to those who wish to explore it,
leaving them free to choose how far down into the
Underworld they want to go. And also not to force
those who have other interests in life to make this

journey. Personal computers should be seen and not heard—just be there when you need them.

This begins with integrated circuits. Wozniak and Jobs took special pride in building machines that maximize the usefulness of a deliberately—even passionately!—reduced number of components. In 1976, the Apple II was a masterpiece containing 130 integrated circuits that did more than machines with twice that number. The Macintosh with its 53 circuits does more, better, than others with 250.

A passion for technical elegance, to be sure. But not only that. It's also a way of bringing down the cost, which makes the product competitive. Another advantage is the functional reliability, which is always directly linked to the number of components. If you have fewer components you can do without a fan that might break down or short-circuit and cause a poorly protected machine to fry.

Things didn't always happen so easily before today, when there is a docile personal computer within everyone's personal reach. Because of the dizzy speeds of computers, time-sharing was invented. In the early days the high cost of the first computers meant that they had to be used intensively, and since the fixed overhead was higher than salaries, people got used to operating them around the clock. An old idea handed down from the industrial age: equipment investment must be made to pay off. Just like at auto factories, the employees worked three shifts. Their actions were repetitive—like those on an automobile assembly line—feeding batches of punched cards into the machine. The external memory was stored in a card hopper containing the program and the data—often very complicated software that makes Basic look childishly simple. This software fed the computer information for processing the data or activating an internal program. Very soon afterward, in the fifties, to avoid shipping cards from one city to another, they invented a card reader that connected to a telephone. Then they realized that a computer capable of running a million operations per second was connected to far slower printers that printed only ten characters per second, representing a considerable time loss. So the idea was born of making them do other tasks during printing—in particular, serving several users at a time. More precisely, the computer serves each user in turn, but the turns last only a tenth of a second, giving the illusion of simultaneity. A juggler who keeps five apples in the air gives the impression of not touching them. When computers work for several people at a time, we call it time-sharing. But sometimes they can be overwhelmed, like a waiter trying to serve beer to everyone at the same time. Time-sharing has its limitations, and personal computers have largely surmounted them.

People quickly got used to the phenomenal speeds. After a few weeks at the computer, your sense of time changed and there were complaints of having to wait three seconds for the computer to do its work. I tend to get impatient if the printer on my Macintosh doesn't spit out a page *right now*, even though I've used graphics and special fonts. I'm spoiled by my personal computer.

The user can be only partially aware of all these complex phenomena going on inside the computer. The level of complexity has become such that no one can apprehend it in its totality. Even the programmer sees only part of the picture, and the machines are only programmable at all because it is possible to address one stage of their complicated structure at a time, one intellectual model, without keeping track of all the possible paths and nestings.

The particular charm of the Macintosh is that it is the most refined example of the interpenetration of hardware and software. It has an additional stage: basic software that exists nowhere else and that gives it its personality. The motor, or microprocessor, receives marching orders that are transmitted to "dead" memories called ROMs (read-only memories). These dead memories contain this basic software, which is protected by a copyright similar to that of literary and artistic property. What happens? The microprocessor, the motor, has only fairly rough instructions: it understands orders, which are sequences of ones and zeros given by the hand of the user who moves the "mouse," presses a key, etc. But the Macintosh has rather sophisticated instructions that allow it to do a lot of things with great simplicity. How does it get from one to the other? Through the basic software, also called the operating system, which serves as a translator, a bridge. It is in fact a semihardware layer, a logical Jell-O. We speak of crystallization when we talk about it. In fact it is neither software nor hardware, but firmware, and it is the firmware talking when the Macintosh greets its user with the "happy Mac" symbol. Then, when you use a program like MacWrite, the program transmits the instructions to the firmware. Each program leans on this support when it starts to run. All the graphics, text, and manipulative possibilities of the Macintosh are contained in two little chips of firmware whose intellectual richness is incalculable. They took hundreds of thousands of hours of research to develop. This is one of the foundations of the Macintosh. The microprocessor is replaceable; any dealer can supply one. But the firmware is intellectual property to which we have kept the rights. It is because of its presence, for example, that Apple II diskettes cannot be used on the Macintosh—they don't know how to communicate with it. The format could be made to fit and the set of instructions rewritten, but it is probably impossible to adapt them so that they can have a coherent relationship with the firmware.

In a way, it resembles writing. When you write,

you're not always aware of the different mechanisms you're using. To program you have to work on a simplified model since excess information about what is going on would give the creator "writer's block." So the designer must give the programmer intellectual tools that he can master, and the success of a program will be closely linked to the simplicity of the images he produces: a sheet of paper with columns, paint brushes, pencils. . . .

Talent means choice. Knowledge is organized in layers by stages of complexity, like those Russian dolls that nest inside each other. At each stage, the man there mobilizes his particular abilities and combines the elements he has available. Needless to say, this way of going about things makes it impossible to work in isolation. It takes teamwork (if there is such a thing) to design a computer.

What happens between the machine and the person using it? The machine transmits its encoded messages into a language intelligible to the human brain. It is not a horizontal translation, like that of an Italian text translated into Spanish, but a vertical translation between a relatively simple organism—the machine—and an infinitely more complex organism—the human brain. The difference in complexity between the two is vertiginous—literally unthinkable. It is of the order of one inch to seven thousand miles—the distance from Paris to Cupertino, California. The complexity of the human brain is actually incomprehensible. Billions of neurons each create thousands of connections to form a topology, a labyrinth impossible to imagine, to conceive. The difference between the computer and the brain is such that the gap is not merely quantitative but qualitative, and this gap is a given for anyone thinking about what we call artificial intelligence. Computers will not compete with man tomorrow, or the day after tomorrow.

Even with this basic handicap, there is something in this instrument that upsets and worries us: it extends our thinking. And it does this so well, in its own way, with its peculiar limitations, that you can hardly avoid asking yourself some odd questions. If this machine is thinking better and better, am I, who asks the question, a machine? The operation of the computer supplies images for understanding certain psychological processes. In a book I once read on learning to control one's dreams, it is explained that if you want to remember your dreams you have to lie quite still when you wake up because certain neuromuscular relationships, if activated, have the effect of dumping the short-term memory. If you want to remember the dream stored in the short-term memory you have to give it time to make its way to the long-term memory. Anyone can try this for himself. In computer terms, we might say that you have to dump what is written in the computer memory onto a diskette before switching off the machine. Then you can leave it there without worrying about it because you can always find it again.

There is another disturbing relationship between the computer and the living person. It is often said that one definition of living is the creation from small phenomena of large, highly organized phenomena: the ovum and the sperm create a man weighing 150 pounds. An assassination in Sarajevo triggered a world war. With the computer, a touch as soft as a butterfly's wing also triggers organized effects on a large scale.

By the way, I want to tell computer users who have gone through the painful experience of inadvertently losing what they had forgotten to back up that they are neither the first nor the last; it has happened an incalculable number of times, and it's as useful as it is inevitable. Indeed, good computer manuals are those that ask, "Did you make this error?" The right answer is "Yes," because it is the only one that will enable the user to get to the next part of the manual.

When I get asked by people on the defensive just what computers are for, I recognize their concern as being my own as well. It is not linked to ignorance but to anxiety, to exasperation at the imagined rivalry that the too-perfect performance of these machines can represent. Anxiety is the opposite of fascination, and no one is immune. But I know that as long as computers are incapable of playing with words and figures of speech (metonymies, syllepses, puns), there can be no rivalry.

It is difficult to see how the complexity of the human brain could be transferred into a code or program, however complicated. There exist, in mathematics, problems recognized as insoluble because the solution would take more stages than there are elementary particles in the universe. It's like a drawing of a network of four or five intersecting roads with three cars driving along such that if one car is on a particular segment of road the second must not be on another given segment, and so on. It seems childish, and yet there is no general solution to this type of problem, no formula, no algorithm that can take account of all the data. It is possible to state this problem but not to solve it. Likewise it is impossible to draw a map of the human brain. Perhaps this is the type of problem we have: insoluble. Reality probably has limitations that thought does not. Of course you can say the words "a map of the human brain," but there is no reality that corresponds to these words.

Many sciences are trying the experiment of descending into the abyss, like the two mirrors facing each other a short distance apart that reflect the same image to infinity. Those drawings that represent a drawing that represents . . . , etc. There is always another Russian doll, another nest. Scientists working on particle physics have made discoveries of this kind, and it's impossible to imagine where it will all end unless—and this is doubtful, to say the least—we find the ultimate components of matter from which the whole structure is built.

Information theory contains another paradox: information—whose very nature it is to be transmitted—degrades precisely when it is transmitted. To transmit a piece of information is to inject noise, or entropy, into it. This mystery turns up in biology. At the lowest molecular level—the electronic level—of man, we find information stored in DNA, but this information necessarily degrades during transmission. There remains the question of how life evolved, fabricated information despite this degradation, and produced sense despite entropy.

It is thus possible to face situations in which logic demonstrates logically its own contradictions. Science, faced with these questions, helps us to recognize the component of the absurd contained in reality. What is fascinating about computers is that by their very limitations they teach us about part of our own functioning. It's another feedback effect. They sell so well because the desire they whet is fueled by an ambivalence, a question: Will this thing do my thinking for me or will I manage to dominate it? When you take the plunge and turn on a computer, you notice with relief that it stays in its assigned place— the instrumental, subordinate place for which it was designed. It's not a rival but a servant. When you have truly understood and experimented with this arrangement, you have the intoxicating feeling of controlling a huge amount of power.

It's not easy to be a human, i.e., an object that examines itself. It creates all sorts of labyrinths, descents into the abyss, uncertainties, and guilt. But this doubtful privilege is also a rather reassuring certainty when we look at the computer universe. It's really hard to see how a computer could become aware of its own existence. At the end of the film *2001* there's a disturbing scene in which the computer, Hal, regresses and pleads for its life while its neurons are being unplugged. But today, and for as far into the future as imagination can foresee, it is inconceivable that a machine could feel itself to be alive. We can formulate the same idea backwards: if no machine knows that it is alive, no machine can know that it is dead. By contrast it can happen that I, a human, imagine that I'm a machine. You can, for example, represent destiny in the form of a program, awareness in the form of an algorithm. An algorithm is a set of steps describing in advance something one is going to do. If I'm an algorithm I no longer have free will; I am dead. When you embark on this kind of speculation you're likely to get a little dizzy.

Certain scientists are very attached, for poorly explained reasons, to a reductionist concept of the mind that makes it the result of neurobiological processes. Faced with the infinitesimal components of matter, the frontiers of life become imprecise; there are certain viruses that we cannot assign to either the class of crystals or that of organisms. The next stage along this line of thinking is to give them a molecular and hence electronic origin. Take another step, and you explain the mind in terms of quantum mechanics. But according to quantum mechanics, the very presence of mind in the conscious observer influences and makes finally indeterminate whatever phenomena are observed. If I'm not an algorithm I can't be fully described, enclosed in a system. So our epistemological reasoning comes full circle.

As you can see, being around computers has devastating effects on those of us who are sensitive to shivers of logic. I see I have written that computers are dead machines while all day long I talk of them as if they were living beings!

11

Beauty and Function

ROLAND BARTHES WAS ONE OF THE FIRST to sense and express it magnificently in *Mythologies*, about the Citroën DS19: technology produces art. Clearly, these machines are works of art in themselves; not just because they are beautiful and well packaged, but also because of their internal design, the harmony of their invisible structures. A little Sony Walkman, a Terraillon scale, or a Coca-Cola bottle—objects that have their own special beauty, even if they are turned out by the millions. For me, personal computers embody this quality in an even more fascinating way, probably because it is reinforced by their element of mystery: no one knows exactly what they are capable of. Their specific beauty is continually evolving and never reveals itself entirely.

What so often prevents us from recognizing their aesthetic quality is the outdated concept that a work of art must be unique. These modern works are reproduced by the thousands, by the millions, but they nonetheless carry an idea within them; they have a unique shape, transmitting the intuition of their creator.

Steve Jobs had a vision. When he hired Harmuth Esslinger, the designer of the Porsche 928, he knew what he wanted: he wanted Apple products to stop being just machines and become works of art. This was probably the best way of magnifying their somewhat magical quality and making it visible to the naked eye.

Esslinger's first masterpiece was the plastic body for the compact Apple II. He began by changing its color, creating a machine in a highly elegant textured color called Snow White, with a beautiful separate screen. The consequences of this minor revolution surprised everyone. In parallel, our advertising became more sober and spare; the Apple name became more discreet: instead of fitting into the bite in the apple against a black or multicolored background, it was written below the logo; the cartons were redesigned in white. . . . A strong idea can be recognized because it draws others in its wake. There were very few changes after that, even when the Apple *IIe* came out, with fewer components, which could have allowed more freedom in the design of the case. But someone in the company intuitively felt that the line should not be changed because it would impair the identity of the object. We must not commit the same error as Volkswagen with its 1600 model, which customers found ho-hum by comparison with the Rabbit.

I have to admit that the design of the Macintosh was less of an achievement. It was done by a disciple of the 1950-ish Raymond Loewy school. By itself it looks rather elegant, and it's vertical, whereas most personal computers are horizontal. But when you examine it closely you notice useless moldings and a spatula mark around the edge of the keyboard, details that give it a rather old-fashioned air even though it came out in 1984. The first machine designed by Esslinger appeared three months after the creation of the Macintosh and immediately made the Loewy-influenced design look a little dated. Tastes change in mysterious ways. In ten years these machines will probably look like postwar refrigerators, but in ten more they will be classics, like the jukeboxes that are coming back into fashion today.

If they are to live, objects must be designed as much for pleasure as for efficiency. A car isn't used just to get around, but to affirm one's identity. If this were not so, everyone would be driving Dodge Aspens, and we would see fewer fine, sophisticated cars. Clothes are not just for keeping out the cold, but for showing oneself to one's best advantage. A library is not just for storing books but for reading. A stereo system is not just for listening to perfect sounds, but for dreaming while listening to music. They are instruments for pleasure—a fact all too seldom recognized. To convince yourself, take a look at what happens in societies where pleasure is viewed with suspicion: such objects are rare and costly, sometimes even forbidden. There is one domestic copy of the Apple II in the Soviet Union. It is called the Agat, it costs $16,000, and no one can own one without government authorization any more than one can possess a photocopier. Why do French cars so rarely have automatic transmissions when automatics are so much easier to drive? Because there is a special pleasure—phallic, virile—in shifting gears on the floor, and customers prefer a manual gearbox. Ergonomic discourses on the correct rules for locating the elements of a machine tend to neglect this aspect of things, yet it is a fundamental one.

It is high time to question the old religious notions that, ever since Adam and Eve were expelled from Paradise, have associated work with unhappiness. Perhaps early Christians agreed that the birth of Christ must be placed in the darkest month of the year because one must suffer first to obtain one's eternal reward. I often notice the pained expressions of people when I tell them my job is fun. To get pleasure out of working appears shocking because it contradicts the basic laws of religion. For work to be valuable, it must be painful.

But this commandment—"In sorrow shalt thou bring forth children," etc.—is perhaps only the outcome of circumstances of biological evolution that no longer have a raison d'être. Before the pill, "illegitimate" sexual pleasure involved the risk of unwanted children; by extension we were saying that to have pleasure you had to have fear. It was not possible, and therefore "not right," to enjoy oneself fearlessly. The pill removed the fear, but the old guilt reflexes often continue to govern behavior. It takes time for the traces to evaporate.

In the same way, throughout the millennia of human history, man had to labor—plow, sow, reap, mow, store, hunt, forge—to survive. It was natural to accept this state of affairs as man's destiny. But we're coming into a time when, thanks to technology—farm machinery, machine tools, washing machines, etc.—it is possible to dissociate the two for the first time. The link between unhappiness and work, like that between joy and risk, is no longer inevitable. But we behave as if our memories were imprinted by these associations of ideas, as if we were unable to accept the idea that these old contingencies, because they have been promoted to the rank of ethical imperatives, have no foundation in reality. Nothing is more difficult than to give up suffering.

Sometimes there's a traffic slowdown on the freeway because of an accident. Even when the cause of the slowdown has disappeared, the freeway retains the memory of the accident for quite a long time. We must now realize that the freeway is clear. Prophets of doom notwithstanding, it *is* possible to work with beautiful machines. And there is no law to prevent it.

12

This Idiot Savant

IS IT POSSIBLE TO REPRODUCE supposedly intelligent human behavior with a machine? In other words, is artificial intelligence a dream, a possible stage of progress, or a danger that threatens us? In a field that encourages heady or inspired lucubrations, there are three approaches: pragmatism, which dominates the English-speaking countries; dogmatism, which is wreaking havoc in France; and espionage, which saves the Soviet countries the trouble of repeating research that has already been done.

There is one infallible way to find out whether a machine is intelligent or not. It is the test of Turing, the English mathematician whose biography was recently published and who constructed some of the foundations of information science. You put a ma-

157

chine and a man in two rooms next to each other. The man doesn't know "who" is in the adjacent room. They communicate by keyboard without seeing each other. If the man asks the machine questions and, from its responses, cannot divine that it is a machine he's talking to, the machine is intelligent. This is the best definition of artificial intelligence: the impossibility of distinguishing it from human intelligence.

Now, what characterizes the human mind is a strange combination of rigor and lack of rigor that allows the elastic deformation of concepts. All the tricks of rhetoric, for example, are deformations of concepts on the model of metonymy, which consists of using a word to mean something else. Intelligence is the miraculous functioning of an enormous network of poorly swept, rutted, twisting roads filled with obstacles. We are only scratching the surface when it comes to understanding how the mind works. How, for example, do we encode puns, humor, or figures of speech such that a computer can integrate them? How can we translate into binary numbers a language we call intuition and which consists of thinking about a problem without knowing all the data?

Creation of artificial intelligence assumes that we are fairly well aware of all these mechanisms, so that we can reduce them to a binary system, which is the basis of computer science, in a sufficiently elaborate way for this binary system to restore phenomena in all their complexity. It is true that the functioning of the nervous system is itself binary-based, because it is composed of neurons switching alternately on and off. But this binary nature does not suffice for a meaningful description of the nervous system. In fact, the problem of artificial intelligence is that of a qualitative mutation. We do not even know whether this mutation takes place in the human brain, starting with a particular number of neurons or as a function of other parameters. We do not know when and how the accumulation of quantity creates a qualitative jump. We currently lack a way of conceptualizing it. For the moment, we content ourselves with living it every day.

The transition from the third to the fourth generation of computers did not raise this question of qualitative mutation. Today we are living with fourth-generation computers: this simply means that we have gone from integrated circuits to large-scale integrated circuits because circuits have become more compact. But the transition to a hypothetical fifth generation would be a qualitative change. We can imagine it, but there is no reason to believe that it is probable or even possible. I don't think we can reproduce, or even comprehend, the nervous system. At the present time, research is being done into expert systems and inference engines: they are given some basic knowledge and rules for combining the elements of this knowledge. But in no way, as things stand at present, is a computer capable of inventing a new idea, making a pun, or constructing a chain of reasoning that goes beyond what it has stored in memory.

In five years or less, computers will probably be capable of recognizing handwriting. We will have taken one step forward in understanding the mystery of shape recognition. No one knows today what intellectual operation or algorithm allows us to reliably recognize a face, a voice, someone's handwriting. There are complex shapes that we can describe fairly completely but without being able to recognize them definitely. This is the case with a sophisticated assembly of polygons that can be described in Cartesian terms without omitting anything. But if we introduce slight differences between two assemblies of this type, the human eye could not pinpoint these differences with any certainty. In the same way, today we can describe a fingerprint even though the eye cannot distinguish its details.

Conversely, there are shapes that everyone recognizes immediately and with certainty, but cannot describe exhaustively. A music lover definitely recognizes a Mozart sonata, a Bach fugue, or a Chopin nocturne. He could never describe exactly what allows him to identify them with such certainty. This recognition, which is obvious to us, entirely escapes the computer, which cannot recognize Chopin, Bach, Mozart, or the face of my news vendor. Once again we are confronted with the mystery of quality.

The computer is a very fast idiot savant that runs through a number of options very rapidly and allows us to extend the range of our intelligence, but it does not have the encompassing glance that allows us to recognize a shape. This is because, at the present state of our knowledge, we are unable to break down this process of shape recognition into a complex chain of elementary conditions.

What is more, we do not know what "sense" is, either. Imagine a computer sensitive to the human voice. I tell it: "It's eight o'clock." This computer will eventually learn how to transform this wave of sound into a character string. It will write on its screen: "it apostrophe ess space eight space o apostrophe clock." Does this mean that the character string will make sense to the computer? Not at all. From sound signals we have obtained alphabetical characters, which is already quite a feat. Psychoacoustics has made some progress, and we can design computers that will be 99 percent successful in recognizing a speaker, always the same one, with a vocabulary of a few hundred words. But we cannot say that the computer understands what it is doing, or even that it is conscious of communicating with us, of being in the presence of someone. Go tell a computer: "You know, I saw this amazing guy the other day on TV. . . ." What gives language its savor is precisely its approximation.

No one is anxious to speak "correctly" to a computer, i.e., always to use the same words to say the same thing. If the programmed code for asking the machine to discard a document is "discard" you can't say "discard this paper" or "don't forget to throw that stuff into the trash" or "I'm fed up with that thing." For this type of simple instruction, the use of gesture and picture—the Macintosh mouse for example—are infinitely preferable to words.

It is not obvious that the recent manufacture of computers with synthetic voices is perceived as true progress by the users. Owners of "talking cars," after the novelty has worn off, often feel uneasy and tend to switch the speaking mechanism off. The production of speaking domestic appliances has fallen markedly in recent years. And speech-recognizing machines have fared no better: users have found, for example, that it is far easier to press a button that says "120°" than to articulate distinctly, "Temperature equals one hundred and twenty degrees." When we translate everything into language, we forget that we also express ourselves with our bodies and our hands.

At the present time, these speech techniques have very limited applications. They are useful, for example, in sorting luggage at airports or security stations. An employee watches the suitcases go by on a conveyor and reads out the labels, which the computer doesn't know how to do, and informs the computer of their destinations: "Bombay! San Francisco!

Nice!" Nothing very glorious about this: paradoxically we're back in the situation where human employees have to make up for the deficiencies of computers and revive boring jobs like subway ticket-punchers.

For something to make sense there must be someone else there. It's the same with desire . . . desire, sense, beauty, the music of Chopin, the face of a woman—they're *indescribable.* How do we get from the sign to the sense and finally to speech and art? These questions involve areas outside the universe of computers: they have a different nature. The problem of artificial intelligence is closely linked to this enigma: the transition from quantity to quality. Discerning sense, recognizing a shape—these are incredibly complex operations that the human brain, this mechanism developed over billions of years, can carry out spontaneously. It would be highly presumptuous to imagine that in five, ten, or fifty years we would manage to reproduce as complex an object as the brain, and give our computers antennas as sensitive as our eyes or hands.

How do we go from the discontinuous to the continuous? If you take a large regular polygon and cut off all the corners one by one, it gets smoother and smoother and finally becomes a circle. The famous Zeno's Paradox is a logical curiosity about the transition from the continuous to the discontinuous: if Achilles never catches up with the tortoise, it's because the tortoise is always infinitesimally ahead of him. But in fact we know very well that in life, in the continuum of life, Achilles will catch up with the tortoise. So it is sometimes more realistic, more accurate, to reason fuzzily rather than precisely. Thinking in small fractions decreasing to infinity can lead to absurdities. Between the two logical orders there is a qualitative difference.

Having learned to think in continuities, it is very difficult for us to have to take into account, through quantum physics for example, the disagreeably discontinuous and counter-intuitive nature of the world. In the computer world, we go from the one to the other every day because for each program, for each new application, we have to work out a translation between these two categories of thought.

Computers will help us settle all those impassioned debates on content and form. What they teach us about intelligence is that you don't have to choose between cheese and dessert; you can have them both! The mystery of intelligence arises precisely from the impossibility of distinguishing between content and form, between structure and matter. Thinking about intelligence means thinking about the topological paradox which says that a concept is a path between two places—two concepts—and that this path itself becomes a new place that will have links with the first two.

———

There was a boy in my high school who knew by heart the scores of all the first-division soccer games over the previous five years. There are people who collect swizzle sticks and baseball cards. This is compulsive collecting, not too far removed from the work a computer can do. And yet the accumulation of knowledge is necessary for anyone who wants to see forms emerge, who wants to understand: if you want to trace the pattern of this century's history, you have to know what event occurred.

Likewise, in mathematics, you can't follow the reasoning unless you have a good collection of theorems. An infinitely intelligent being who had no memory would have to start at the bottom each time with some basic axioms to solve elementary problems: each time he had to unplug a sink he would have to reinvent a series of interlocking theorems to work out the physics of the wrench for unscrewing the pipe.

For human beings knowledge, like economics, is inseparable from affect. This is what makes computers so radically different. Psychoanalysts have demonstrated the intricate relationships between libido and knowledge. All memorizing methods are based on exercises that have something to do with using affect to jog the memory. If you want to memorize a list of names, the most efficient way is to associate each name with a stage on the route you take to walk to school every day. Failure to recognize this affective dimension of knowledge is at the base of many misunderstandings and arguments.

In a recent book, there is this tale, by Jacques Seguela, of a Japanese schoolboy: The children had been asked to say what snow becomes when it melts. The schoolboy replied, "It becomes spring." An inspired reply if ever there was one . . . but the child was dismissed from school because his reply wasn't what was expected of him. Yet what he had said was precisely what artificial intelligence, in the wildest dreams of the engineers, would like to make a computer capable of: inventing a poetic response. The drama stems from the fact that all knowledgeable people tend to believe that the knowledge they possess is unique and the best kind, the only kind that lets you succeed in life. It is aberrations of this type that make knowledge a privilege instead of a pleasure, and that's what sterilizes it.

In France, especially at the top, people have the idea that the only route to success is through a certain school. Go to the Polytechnique, the Mining Institute, École Centrale, or the ENA (National School of Government). Then you can be sure you'll know enough and you can put your knowledge to work. *But one never knows enough.*

This prejudice is the result of the ossification of structures in a society that for a long time has grown by refusing to look at anything that might endanger it. It runs counter to the economic revolution that is changing some fundamentals—the very role of producing objects, for example. In one hundred years, agriculture, which used to employ 80 percent of the working population, has become a minority activity. Currently 1.5 percent of the U.S. population is able to feed every American and a few Russians. It looks as though an identical transformation will reduce the role played by manufacturing physical objects in economic activity. In the coming years, we will be witnessing similar phenomena with the automation of factories: only a few skilled workers will be needed to produce ten of thousands of Walkmen, automobiles, Macintoshes.

But what we will never succeed in satisfactorily automating are services: information, communication, all the fields where affect plays an essential part. The American astronauts saw this when their monkeys went on a hunger strike, and all they needed to do to get them to eat was feed them by hand.

Generalized corporatism is an avatar of this rigidity in French society that not only refuses to take these profound changes into account, but freezes up before them as if it were desirable or even possible to halt them. Every profession, from podiatrist to doctor, from grocer to lawyer to pharmacist, claims its own charter, safeguards, and barriers against the rest of the world. Each one defends its little square of territory with the retrograde idea that knowledge confers rights, while the opposite could very well be argued—that knowledge creates obligations.

From this point of view, the personal computer, because it is distributed (unlike mainframes) outside institutional circuits, is a disturbing element in the great corporate structure. It develops personal power, it opens a direct path to different modes of knowledge, it relativizes the power of intermediaries: teachers, specialists, owners, intercessory priests. Some companies like IBM, by giving training seminars, have attempted to preserve this intermediary function of the institution, to hang onto this power which for so long was the other side of the coin of knowledge: "It's too complicated for you; call our customer department and we'll be happy to help you. . . ." The customers know very well that these elitist speeches are out of touch with the times. At Apple we listen to them with a wicked chuckle: they are the basis of our success.

I have often regretted that I never finished my doctorate in science. I am, as they say in the United States, a dropout. In France they look down on you when you haven't collected a few degrees. For a long time I felt stigmatized by my identity as a mathematician wandering around in the business world. It took me a while to realize that I had been lucky in being forced to earn a living and choose the career that interested me. I regretted, for example, that I had not succeeded in understanding certain rather abstract geometrical concepts. I told myself that without a good teacher I'd never manage it, that I wasn't talented enough. This kind of regret is highly stimulating and leads you to accomplish a lot of things.

I remember my exultation when I noticed that I was continuing to learn. I often meet people who never went to college and get along very nicely. When you get your degree you get the feeling that you've finished your education. You've learned a certain number of things and you can put the books away. My old pre-college math buddies went on to the Polytechnique, and many of them became weapons engineers. It's the shortest path from *A* to *B*. But my thirst for knowledge was never quenched—on the contrary. When I joined Hewlett-Packard France, I rolled up my sleeves; I thought I had to work on numerical analysis. Then I realized this wasn't the right track, but on the way I picked up a new enthusiasm that has never left me.

Then I stopped preferring "hard" sciences to "soft" sciences. En route, for instance, by reading Douglas Hofstadter's book *Gödel, Escher, Bach*, I realized that the "hard" sciences were not as strong as people thought. What does Gödel's famous theorem say? Simply this: a logical system of whatever kind cannot be consistent—free of contradictions—unless

169

it contains at least one proposition that cannot be shown either to belong or not to belong to this system. In a consistent system there is always at least one uncertain proposition. Thus, when a system is consistent it is necessarily incomplete. Conversely, when a system is complete it is necessarily inconsistent. To a Cartesian mind fed on mathematics, Gödel's theorem causes an earthquake. He sets the limits of logic, he reveals the path between the two orders of knowledge, he shows that the edifices of reasoning are often built on sand. He compels a certain humility before the possession of knowledge.

So from that time on I understood that action is also one of the paths of knowledge. And now I know that I can continue to learn outside school, and that this possibility will remain open all my life for as long as I want it open. When I watch fifty year olds crowing over their Macintoshes I realize that they are feeling the sensation I know so well and of which I never tire: the feeling of suddenly having access to domains from which one felt excluded forever. An incomparable sense of freedom—as if their lives had become vast, a limitless space in which they can explore unknown lands containing immense resources. The adventure of knowledge. What could be better?

13

The Code of Life, the "Life" of Computers

EACH GENERATION PRODUCES ITS BUZZWORDS. We in the eighties are obsessed by the word *code* because it designates a concept at the heart of the two breakthrough areas of knowledge: information science and biology. To ordinary people, biology is about life and information science is about machines. But there is a balancing act going on at the very frontiers of life. Computers, those magical objects, give you the feeling they are on the point of being able to think—that they are becoming more alive. On the other hand, biology seems more and more about to die. To begin with, biologists tried to discover how life started, then take care of it, give it, protect it. Today, however, they are trying to elucidate the operation of the genetic code and observe how amino acids do this coding at the genetic level; what they are discovering, as they study life, is the transmission of information. In the strictest sense, *to inform* means to give a form or a shape. The very word *life* is taking on a new meaning. Cellular differentiation, one of the most fascinating phenomena in biology, is contained in the genetic code.

This is what determines the mechanisms by which cells multiply to form the nervous system, skin, bones. In some ways the genetic code is like a tape recording: it contains a certain number of bits forming a sequence that contains the code of the human being as he is manufactured. The idea of making identical doubles, or clones, followed this discovery. But we are also the product of our environment, and we know that to make a true clone we would also have to reproduce its parents, cousins, friends, bosses. In a famous demonstration, Lewis Thomas showed that to clone a man we would have to clone the entire world.

Taking this limitation into account, there remains what computer science and biology have in common: the code, the program. If the cell were a computer, its genetic code would be the program. But genetic engineering is confronted with questions far more disturbing than those posed by computer science. Research in biology has brought us to the point where we have to decide when the embryo becomes a person. And we can no longer ignore the fact that genetic engineering, which is now capable of *changing life*, may have devastating repercussions for the world in which we live.

Having said that, as an indefatigable optimist I remain attentive to progress in biology. Researchers have hopes of discovering the herpes or common cold vaccine and of eradicating a number of viral diseases by means of bacteria whose genetic code they have managed to alter. Just as a skilled technician can get inside a computer program and change it, biologists are learning to alter the genetic codes of bacteria to make them produce drugs like interferon or antibodies. Biologists are on the verge of prolonging and improving our lives by learning about the mechanisms of aging. Perhaps diseases of the muscular or skeletal systems linked to senility or menopausal disorders will one day disappear. But it is inevitable that in these fields the hopeful factors are always offset by causes for anxiety.

The very research that will improve our lot is the same research that may lead to bacteriological warfare and the temptations of omnipotence paving the terrifying path of genetic selection. I have often asked when scientists would take the dizzying step of applying to human beings the same methods they use in breeding horses. Technically, it will be possible to choose, modify, and replace genes. Here again the positive applications are inseparable from the dangers: the genetic code of a human embryo could be inspected and genes containing future malformations could be rectified. A gene for bowlegs or squinting? It will be tempting to repair it at the very start of life . . . and what a saving for Medicare! These questions are infinitely more disquieting than those thrown up by computer science. They contain within them the seeds of totalitarian temptation.

Today computers are used by biologists like any other tool. Computer designers, however, do not make ready use of biology as a tool—at least, not yet. But we may imagine that some day in the future, progress in miniaturizing computer circuits will be blocked just because it is no longer possible to make any more refinements in silicon etching, which is something like lithography, to create smaller and smaller circuits. When that day comes, something else will have to be found. It would be inconceivable for research just to stop: it would be as if writers stopped producing new books because the presses could not go any faster. We still have quite a way to go with present-day materials. Circuits will not necessarily become denser, but they will certainly become more efficient. It will probably no longer be possible to quadruple the size of memories every four years, as happened in the fifties. When I joined Apple, we were going from 16K to 64K memories. At present a Mac+ can hold 1,000K, or one megabyte. In four years, memories will be another four times denser, which means that only one-fourth the number of chips will be needed for the same memory size or the same number of chips will make a memory four times as large. But as soon as the limit of density permitted by chip lithography is reached, inventors will probably turn to biology, which can give them organic circuits with an infinitely larger space for the memory.

An important step will have been taken. A single living cell has more memory capacity than many very large computers. This reciprocal enrichment of technologies is only science fiction today. We can imagine fairly well how it will come about, but it is probably no more realistic than imagining a computer capable of passing the famous Turing test of artificial intelligence.

Today the most nightmarish threats as well as the most decisive progress are coming from biology. Computer science contributes to the progress of "knowledge tools." Biology contributes to the progress of life. However, biology has not undergone to the same degree the acceleration that marked the recent history of computers. Progress in genetics has been slower than expected. A few years ago they were predicting in Silicon Valley that computer science would be overtaken by bioengineering, and that there would be an explosion of discoveries. This explosion has not taken place for a very simple reason: you can easily do strange things in testing a computer, but with the products and applications of biology you have far greater limitations in testing. Errors have rather different consequences. In 1968, at Hewlett-Packard, in a fit of homesickness due to the events going on in Paris, I put up in my office a poster reading: "It is urgently necessary to make mistakes." Indeed I have been faithful to this precept. But it's not exactly a slogan biologists could use.

14

The Importance of
Back-and-Forth

ONCE, AS I WALKED DOWN the Boulevard Saint-Michel in Paris, I stopped by a bookstore window to look at the software selling for $2. I mean books, of course. Today a small computer without software costs at least $300 to $450. But software will one day be selling for the price of comic books. We all know that the selling price of a book is largely determined not by the amount of work it took to write but by the number of copies expected to sell in a competitive market. No one would think of spending eighteen dollars today to buy a funny book. They don't even dare to raise the price of the newspaper *Le Monde* to 10 francs ($1.50), which would be a very small price for the sum of effort and thinking it offers every day. Don't get me wrong: I'm not saying a computer program

181

is the same thing as a book—if only because software contains levels of organization and movement that a book does not have. It offers a kind of flexibility and wealth for the imagination. The computer changes the person who uses it, and the user changes the computer in return; it's an exchange that is truly remarkable. It's the back-and-forth that's important. Rarely are you as active when reading a book as when working with a computer.

Computers will multiply the amount of knowledge that is immediately accessible. When we are able to fit hundreds of thousands of dictionary pages onto optical disks the size of a CD, this will not be miniaturization—it will be an explosion. At Carnegie-Mellon they have already started to do simulations of this type. Using a Macintosh connected to a large computer that acts like the library of Alexandria, you can call up a Shakespeare play and the bibliographic references to it, read the books referred to, then come back to the initial text. It allows you to browse, to operate by associations of ideas in a way natural to the human mind. These techniques will allow us to connect one piece of knowledge to another with the same ease we have in associating ideas. When a machine has four to ten times the memory capacity of a present-day Macintosh, forty times its disk capacity, and ten times its speed in the same package, things will happen that are scarcely imaginable. There will be a qualitative leap, not linked to increased speed alone. This machine could store longer texts, work faster, respond better to a gesture. A writer working on the synopsis of a book could at the same time consult a Washington *Post* article. Today I can read the Washington *Post* computer abstracts every morning at home. I have a list of fourteen hundred information utilities that offer me services, information, and contacts from a distance. There's something for every special-interest group, from car enthusiasts to gurus. The beauty here is that many changes which will be brought about by increased power and capacity are unpredictable. No one can describe what has not yet been invented. What is certain is that there will be Macintoshes the size of a large book that you can carry around and set on your lap to work under a tree.

What is unique about the personal computer is the interaction it fosters with its user: both are changed by one another during the course of an activity. Printing was the first revolution in communications. Its effect was to automate and make more productive a job that thus far had been the burden and the privilege of medieval scribes. The idea was always to produce a one-way text, from the originator to the recipient. The revolution of the movies, although it introduced some upheavals with respect to the theater, is also a one-way communication channel. The moviegoer, seated in a dark room, looks at the screen with varying degrees of mental activity.

But the way he looks does not change the film, any more than a reader changes the pages of the book he reads. Obviously television is an even more passive form of communication than the movies because you don't even have to go through the ritual of going out, buying a ticket, finding a seat in the dark, buying popcorn, holding hands with your girlfriend. With a computer it is truly impossible to remain passive. Before the computer, only the telephone had allowed two-way transmission; and even it was originally designed as a simple receiver of sounds. The manufacturers imagined, for example, that they could broadcast concerts by telephone; it was only a precursor of radio. Another surprise in applying technology!

In a dozen years, computers will probably not be more intelligent than they are today. Progress in their intelligence will probably consist of developing expert systems that will let you read the international press or wander at will in the labyrinth of the Library of Congress without leaving your home. They will not be able to write poetry. But they will probably be more charming, loyal, docile, and powerful than any poet could be. They will affirm our nature of being creatures who never cease to learn. We are at the dawn of an era in which computers will allow us to change our life-style radically. I can well imagine that every morning I will wake up to find that my computer has picked up my electronic mail, has given me a selection of information on subjects I want to write about in my next book, and has prepared a summary of the most important information for me. Because they have access to incalculable volumes of information, computers will increasingly serve us as intellectual steering wheels.

Computer science will never be a great job generator. But what we might hope for is that it will free those whose occupations are intellectual from time-wasting, humdrum tasks. By opening unlimited access to the knowledge stored throughout the world, they will prodigiously increase the power of our civilization.

Computers will not find the cure for cancer or hypertension by themselves. But they will definitely make their contribution, simply because they have made the information that already exists available to a larger number of people, so that researchers will not have to repeat experiments. One day, each of us will have access on his screen to hundreds of thousands of book pages and no longer be limited to his own private library. Writers, journalists, company directors, academics . . . all will be working in a totally different way. It is true that setting up data banks poses a new problem: who feeds in the information and by what criteria? Those who draw the navigational maps of these huge libraries will have the power to direct the complicated routes of those who come to read in them. Writing abstracts, indexes, and files is a way of sweeping the paths of knowledge and imprinting them with one's mark. These are obvious dangers, but the dangers are human. They have always existed in other forms—in journalism, for example.

Much has been said about the dangers of putting everyone's personal data into the computer. The danger exists, but it has its own controls. Just as people can distort the nature of information stored in a data bank, they can slide surreptitiously into a conventional filing system to add their two cents. If data banks become widespread, some people will probably take it upon themselves to widen the chinks in the system. They are already at work in the United States: credit bureaus, for example, which keep your credit history on file in case you want to take out a loan, have already been infiltrated by hackers who have managed to break into their files and cook the books. It is not impossible that in a computerized university the same computer whizzes could manage to change their exam grades; the same type of computer fraud is possible with police records, automobile registrations, identity cards, tax records, and so forth.

A system can only be made secure up to a certain point. Locks can be installed to prevent access, but there has to be someone to unlock them in the morning and lock them in the evening, and if this someone has left his key in his pocket it could be copied. The code could be cracked by way of all the time-honored methods: seduction, corruption, blackmail, etc. In fact it's essentially a secrecy problem.

Here we come back to the famous Gödel theorem, according to which a system can be consistent only if it is incomplete. Here, the flaw is human negligence, which can be manifested at two levels: system design and system monitoring. We find the famous problem of *Quis custodiet ipsos custodes?* (Who will guard the guards?), but also this certainty: there are always errors in a program. Why? Perhaps because of the natural distrust human beings have for machines, or the fear of the very idea of perfection, which would remove their control over those machines. But these psychological causes would then only reinforce the logical cause: it is impossible to conceive of a logical system that encompasses all others, just as it is impossible to verify that a large program is perfect. Whatever the case may be, the longer the program, the greater the number of errors. They increase in a proportion that is neither linear, geometric, nor exponential, but combinatory, i.e., faster than exponential. A program can never be guaranteed error-free. A system that would guarantee such perfection is unimaginable. Either the guard is over-fond of chocolate (or blondes), or the programmer has inevitably left at least one error in the system. In any event, perfection of a system is an unattainable absolute, and, when you come right down to it, indeterminism is the best guarantee of freedom.

15

A Second Wind

IN SEPTEMBER 1984, John Sculley asked me to spend a few days in California. He wanted me to head a software publishing division. The former boss of Pepsi-Cola, where he spent seventeen years, a passionate devotee of architecture and electronics, John is a man with whom I am on terms of trust. The best evidence of this is that we still hit it off when we disagree; a conflict of ideas remains a conflict of ideas and never becomes personal. Sculley knows that I have a very clear vision of what Apple could become and that I am ready to dedicate my energy and enthusiasm to accomplishing his goals. He also knows that enthusiasm doesn't stop me from being a manager.

I am convinced that it is time to bring Apple back

to its roots—the roots of the apple tree in blossom. For me, the raison d'être of a company like ours is to succeed in having its customers experience the special joy a good personal computer can give. I believe, as I have said often enough in this book, that the goal has been partially achieved. But there's always a long way to go, and this is what gives the entrepreneur's life its charm. You never really get there: there are always dreams to achieve, new territory to explore. The wonderful thing about innovation is that after a point it becomes mundane, leaving room once more for the novel, the never seen, the unheard of. This continual exploration, this clearing the way for the future is, to my way of thinking, even more necessary in a field where thinking and communications tools are being designed and sold.

The initial talks with John Sculley led to nothing concrete at first but began a process that ended with my being appointed marketing manager for the Macintosh Division in May 1985. Two weeks later I became vice-president for product development. So here I am in the eye of the storm, as it were, in Cupertino, near the city where I had my first love affair with Visicalc. I should add that Apple, like the personal computer industry as a whole, entered 1985 in a crisis period that will lead to some painful changes and, I am convinced, a second wind, a second harvest. (This growth crisis is that of a young tree overladen with fruit and bending under the burden. As

far as I am concerned, it gave a precise objective to
the wish Sculley had had for some time that I go to
California. In a crisis period you don't give in to
dreams or to reality; you neither take refuge in fantasy nor do you crumple under the weight of facts.)

After the discussions of September 1984, Sculley
and I talked about some other projects. Steve Jobs
himself had waved a few rather crazy proposals at
me—like simply taking over his job. Basically, Jobs is
a person who would rather give birth to children than
bring them up, a progenitor rather than a nurse. By
dreaming of handing over the reins, he may have
already been suggesting what finally came to pass:
that he would not continue to manage a company
forever, even one of his own creation. In the end I
had no regrets that these projects were not imple-
mented immediately. I had the time to think about
what such a radical change of life-style would mean
for me.

What I am seeing today is what I have wanted
since 1972, since the day I drove for the first time
down the famous Route 280, "the most beautiful road
in the world" according to Californians, from San
Francisco to Cupertino. I wanted to work there, in a
place where I felt good, where people are welcoming
and determined, where the future is wide open. I
wanted to eat breakfast at 7:00 A.M. at the Good Earth
Restaurant, which smells of cinnamon tea and where
they have the best orange juice in the world. I wanted

to drive through Yosemite on a weekend, to live in this universe of great physical and intellectual spaces where the spirit of adventure and freedom is still so alive. Of course I asked myself whether I could adapt. Once you're over forty your habits become ingrained. But I remembered that I still had three life goals left to accomplish: to write books, to make computers, and one day to have a house in Anjou, that marvelous region of France that lures me with its rocks, houses, roses, wine, and the slightly decadent chateaux you visit on Sundays. I am currently living through the second phase of this program. The people here never make me feel I'm a foreigner: there is no trace of xenophobia in this country of immigrants. And I eventually realized that Sculley had firmly decided to have me come, even if he didn't know what for, and he would do a great deal to bring this about. Now at least, things are far clearer.

There are seven stages in the accomplishment of a project: ignorance, indifference, enthusiasm, panic, searching out the guilty, punishing the innocent, and promoting the nonparticipants. At the time of Apple's restructuring I belonged to the last category. I was the outsider, even though I came from within the company, from Apple France. The outsider can say certain truths and can have a less muddled idea of how to get out of a crisis. This foreignness sometimes creates periods of intense emotion and some privileged moments. But the attraction of these encounters, which is one of the charms of this company, must not make us forget the processes. At Apple, one sometimes tends to forget that life is not made up of a series of orgasms but also of love. The ideal would obviously be to have both.

When people ask me where I'm going to settle I answer: "Somewhere between Cupertino and reality." What did the 1985 crisis tell us? Perhaps that Apple was getting out of touch with its roots—which does not mean that the roots weren't there but that sap wasn't rising any more. Instead of acting out a play for our customers we were acting it for ourselves, for our narcissistic world. And we grew too fat. We gave way to the temptations of corporate politics and institutional egocentrism. In the end, our very identity became fractured and deformed.

What were the signs of the crisis we were going through? Our quarterly sales were $700 million at the end of 1984. These dropped sharply to $400 million in early 1985. We sold 25 percent fewer computers than usual. Apple stock fell from $30 to $17. True, there was a decline in the personal computer industry in general: IBM's profits fell and manufacture of the IBM PC Junior was temporarily halted. Commodore lost money, and companies like Intel and Wang cut back on staff.

But this doesn't mean we can blame the outside world for our troubles. The general situation only exacerbated our internal problems. It is true that we had stopped making Lisa, a decision taken before the crisis, and she disappeared at the very time her sales, under the new name of Macintosh XL, were picking up again. But this decision coincided with the crisis and gave us the bad name of being a company that changes horses in midstream. Apple laid off five hundred people in its factories. One closed down for a week in March 1985. And yet a study published in Infocorp during the same month showed that Macintoshes were outselling all other personal computers.

The product was only part of the problem. What we are witnessing now is a change of epoch. The computer industry has always gone through go-go days with 100 percent annual growth followed by correction phases. We should not exaggerate the seriousness of events: we are going from a world in which projected growth was between 60 percent and 80 percent per annum to a world in which we have to content ourselves with 30–50 percent. This seesaw motion is not due to the whims of fashion: it is a pattern that occurs in any industry at one time or another. After a period when customers are hungry for new products you enter a period when their appetites have to be whetted. The problem is one of perceiving value. For those of us who have a taste for computers, it is easy to perceive the merits of a new product. But those who live only a parallel life with computers have entered a phase of explanation and reflection. In truth, we are emerging from a period when everybody had to have a personal computer and if you didn't have one in your home you were probably old, ugly, impotent, and bald. Fortunately, this blackmail is no longer current. Whatever the qualities of a product, these attacks of hysteria are necessarily followed by a phase of depression in which perspectives change.

We have reached a plateau. The challenge now consists of not only making the best of the situation and launching the machine anew, but also getting it to run at cruising speed without excessive racing or slamming on the brakes. This industry was organized according to sales forecasts that no longer match its capacity. It's time to get into a steady operating mode.

So here I am in Cupertino, under very different circumstances from those I could have imagined when John Sculley made his first proposal in September 1984. At that time I was being considered as someone who would help with growth. Today I am here to create the conditions for future growth by helping Apple to overcome the crisis. Our future depends on our ability to make products that are both serious and exciting, on our determination to develop the technological and software base we have in a systematic manner, to arrange for the existing program libraries to evolve gently by creating more powerful machines that in their turn will spawn new programs—like fir trees, which always have the same color but never the same leaves. We have the classical challenge of the passage from childhood to adulthood. In a period of surging growth you can try all directions and get carried along by the tide, knowing that some mistakes don't count. In a more moderate growth period, compromises with reality become essential. This means that you must stay creative but, in the manner of the professional artist who delivers the commissioned work on time, not in the style of a permanent "happening." To meet this challenge we have one major trump card: Apple has always had a healthy management that has been able to put aside a healthy sum of money. So we're not in the situation of a company that suddenly had to abandon all its dreams. We just have to do some triage.

In the coming years, our products will become more and more themselves by expanding their potential. Apple II—with its slots for interface cards, its modularity, its huge program library, all this potential that the market has pushed us to develop—will acquire more memory, speed, and disk storage capacity, better color, and graphics with better resolution. Macintosh, this child full of promise, will not change its nature either. We will give it brothers that will continue to develop its charm—this intuitive relationship it has with the user because of graphic symbols and responsiveness to hand novements. Because of the large number of programs that have come out over the past three years, we may predict that others will be born which will be even better at revealing what is possible. They will enhance flavors that are already present.

Despite our $2 billion sales volume, we will keep parts of our small-company mentality. If we become more reliable while remaining faithful to our roots, we will achieve the dream of the two Steves, the dream that has become ours.

16

Ten Thousand Libraries of Alexandria*

*This essay is based on a speech given in Boston in August 1986.

WHEN I SIT at my personal computer at the office or at home, I am elated and I am frustrated. I am still impressed by all the doors to new gardens it opens for me, by all the obstacles it removes from my path, by the way it somehow restores to me skills I had lost. My love for computers has withstood the passage of more than a quarter century; it has been well rewarded and will likely grow stronger with time—especially if some of my current frustrations disappear. I am frustrated because there is an irresistible wealth of information and knowledge residing in remote data bases and I cannot get at it. I am frustrated because I can only drool at the thought of visiting and navigating through these ten thousand libraries of Alexandria. They are out there, but I cannot get in.

Today there exists the superficial truth that says you can connect any computer to any other computer. And indeed you can—in theory. This "truth" promises access to remote sources of information: you *can* tap into any remote data base—in theory. The only problem is that each time you change the source of information, the wires and protocol change, and the data structure and user interface also change. Other than that, well, everything is just fine with connecting any computer to any other or with tapping into any remote data base.

Put bluntly, connecting to remote sources of information today is complicated and expensive. You need to be like me—a subsidized hacker—in order to do it. And even so, the technical complexity of the required operations often translates into excessive time spent getting there. So I am, we are, attracted to and frustrated by the rich promise of connecting. Yet we can't ignore the earful we get of the importance of networking computers, connectivity to mainframes, work groups, local-area networks, Ethernet, SNADS, LU 6.2, ISDN, ISO, OSI. . . . Before we drown in the alphabet soup, we should ask what is really in store for us at a time when fewer than 3 percent of all personal computers are networked or connected in a meaningful way. Just what is networking going to do for us? What doors to new gardens will it open? How and how soon?

First of all, we need to see the essential point: networking computers is a means to an end. The really valuable goal is to enable people to share, to reach the fruits of others' work and thoughts. Right now, the technological barriers to this sharing seem to loom very large and to hold much of our attention. But such a focus on nuts-and-bolts problems is a symptom of youth. Our industry and networking technology in particular are immature, and we instinctively look sharply at whatever threatens to stop our eager progress. We're looking in the right direction, though.

And with regard to another sort of focus, we also need to try to see clearly what is implied by the widely enforced connection to the sacred mainframe: thou shalt connect to thy mainframe or be banished to the outer darkness. This threat notwithstanding, for every white-collar worker is a business supported to some extent by a mainframe, there is a genuine benefit: the opportunity to share in the results of collective work stored in the company's computer systems. The threat starts to form here when the mainframe is misrepresented as the sole repository of knowledge and wisdom, as the only library in the world, so to speak. On the contrary, there are a vast number of interesting libraries to visit: Dow Jones, Compuserve,

NEXIS, LEXIS, MCI-Mail, Dialog . . . besides the company's computer systems. This misrepresentation probably stems from confusing two kinds of computing, EDP (electronic data processing) and personal computing. In EDP, the process is in control: individual terminals, work stations, are connected to the mainframe in a virtual master-slave relationship. In personal computing, by contrast, the individual user is in control and freely directs the computer. This freedom extends to which information store he wants to visit, when, and how he wants to browse through it.

Things become a little clearer, a bit more focused, when we realize that we need equal access to three types of networks: the work group, the worldwide interconnection systems, *and* the company-wide information system. Through the work-group network, we can join colleagues to participate in the same projects—untangling a knotted business plan, for instance, or making sense of perplexing marketing data or devising a sales strategy or designing a bridge. The worldwide networks give us maximum diversity: from electronic mail to reference searches in NEXIS or DIALOG. From our homes, we can use these networks to pay the mortgage, summon Washington *Post* stories, look up plane schedules, make reservations, and even order delivery to computer have-nots of paper copies of E-Mail complete with digitized letterhead and signature. And from the company-wide information system, we can get status reports, sales figures, inventories, and more, depending on our need to know and our skill in formulating queries. The obvious differences in these three types of networks should make it clear that we are a long way from the comforting view that "computers are all the same, they just come in different sizes."

Personal computers are valued because they enrich the way we think, organize, communicate, learn, and play. Transparent access to remote information further enriches these activities. A computer with limited memory is like a gifted human being without experience. I want more experience for my personal computer through access to collective memories. But these memories are so big that we have yet to comprehend, to grasp, the effect they will have on us and how we can really make the experience useful. Let me suggest roughly what I mean here with two examples. When I say to you the words "Honda Civic," I can expect you to understand what I have in mind because we almost certainly share closely related cognitive experiences, which are prerequisite for meaningful communication. When I say to you "ten thousand data bases," I have uttered verbal symbols that you can receive and store, but there is no way—at present—for us to put our cognitive arms around them. So truly meaningful communication about the effects of such things can't proceed. Perhaps we have too much information to even get started.

I think the problem is one of lacking navigational tools, handles, links. We are afraid of drowning in a sea of data. What the industry needs to do is build computational wings that will allow us to see the patterns and the currents so that we can swoop down at will for an interesting morsel. This is where what we do with the Macintosh starts to make sense: hand movements and graphics supplement text and keyboard in a two-way communication between man and computer. The computer's strengths compensate for our weaknesses, while we reciprocate with our own unique abilities. The computer tirelessly deals with precise symbol manipulation, reams of numbers, and text; whereas I have a hard time doing sums in my head. But I can recognize patterns, deal with fuzzy or incomplete information, and recognize Mozart in five notes—all of which a computer would have a hard time doing.

The Macintosh makes for a better partnership because it improves the mind-body-computer feedback loop by using graphics and enabling us to speak with our hands. Let me clarify this. To read text or type on a keyboard is to perform an unnatural act; to recognize graphics or speak with our hands is wholly natural because we are genetically "wired" to perform these activities. Graphics allow us temporarily to lose the details and "get the idea," "the big picture," the pattern. Hand movements help us to naturally use navigational tools.

Icons and pointing devices are used in all the current attempts to match large volumes of information to the ways we can most easily comprehend them. An example is Hypertext. Designating ("clicking on") a word or phrase allows us to jump to all associated text, or at least to a window showing the possible links. Following my stream of thoughts, I can be offered bridges from Agincourt to bows and arrows to the art of archery and Zen to Robert Pirsig and motorcycle maintenance and back to Buddha. Hypertext and similar experiments reinforce the point that computers should be made to follow gracefully our ways of thinking and thereby enrich them. Computers, I believe, were created to give us the power to be our best.

In the process of developing sophisticated and natural ways to gain access to huge quantities of information, we will influence the way we work and learn. At work we use personal computers as simulation engines to improve our design of a budget, a presentation, a newsletter, a project schedule, a logic board, or a musical score. A better simulation process allows more parts of the design, more parameters of the necessary decisions, to fit into one human head. Hence, the dual mechanical and creative productivity. Now, imagine that the simulation is gracefully tied to remote data bases and you have an even better simulation. The financial model taps up-to-date information from the commodities market or the company sales history. The presentation and the newsletter get fresh market data before going into print or over the wire.

Learning, building knowledge, also benefits from richer simulations. Knowledge is well-integrated, internalized information that has become available for future freewheeling or tightly controlled thought processes. It is only after I have taken things apart and reconstructed them my own way, several times, that I have effectively integrated knowledge rather than just memorized it. I have built solid links between what I knew and what I just learned in the process of looking at the parts and trying various ways to fit them together.

But all the rich promise of better simulations and graceful ties to remote data bases probably sounds too good to be true—and today it is, for real and frustrating reasons. Still, there is hope. There is desire. We lust for the knowledge accumulated in thousands of data bases around the world. And frustration is a good sign that there exists a real problem for technology to solve (which is always a situation preferable to one in which a vagrant solution goes in search of a problem). The hardest part, because it is a relatively new problem, will be to develop navigational tools. The easiest part will be to remove the expensive inconsistencies in the ways we move information around.

If computers are good at simulation, then surely the computer industry can learn to apply hardware and software to simulate a consistent network of data freeways. Today, however, the situation we have reminds me of travels between France and Spain in the 1950s, when we had to change trains at the border because Spain had a railroad gauge that was incompatible with France's. For the time being, we in the computer industry will have to pay a price to hide the gauge change. But at least we will get at remote information the same way we get at the contents of our local files.

Then something like ISDN (Integrated Services Data Networks) will take over. These are the real, not the make-believe, data freeways. Today the speed limit over residential phone wires and affordable modems is around 2,400 bits per second. ISDN will increase the speed limit by a factor of more than twenty. Our computers will lead better lives; they will have much more animated conversations with remote ones. Instead of more text, they will easily ship beautiful graphics or respond immediately to our request to jump from botulin to Botswana. Even the oldest applications, such as electronic mail, will change. Today most E-Mail networks show their age, besides forcing users to deal with them through a decidedly sovietic interface. Inexpensive high-speed communication will allow us to edit mail on a remote computer the way we do it on a Macintosh today.

Let me close with a few words about specific things to come: the hiding of gauge inconsistencies, which is starting now, will rapidly become better and less expensive; better navigational tools will make commercial debuts in 1987; and ISDN will be ready shortly after 1990. I should stop making predictions because I am well aware of how notoriously unreliable our industry is for delivering on schedule. However, I am confident that my predictions will be fulfilled because more than hope is active here. There is desire.

We are now at an interesting point of transition: we are about to enter the second age of personal computing. Participant and spectator, all I need now is a truly portable Macintosh and a cellular modem so that I can visit some of the ten thousand libraries of Alexandria, do a little research, and then write my next book—all while sitting under a tree.